To Gopi
with love & best wishes
mum & Dad.
your early B'day present
8th Aug 10

THE

TOP 100
CRICKETERS
OF ALL TIME

THE
TOP 100
CRICKETERS
OF ALL TIME

CHRISTOPHER
MARTIN-JENKINS

CORINTHIAN

Published in the UK in 2009 by
Corinthian Books, an imprint of
Icon Books Ltd, Omnibus Business Centre,
39-41 North Road, London N7 9DP
email: info@iconbooks.co.uk
www.iconbooks.co.uk

Sold in the UK, Europe, South Africa and Asia
by Faber & Faber Ltd, Bloomsbury House,
74-77 Great Russell Street, London WC1B 3DA

Distributed in the UK, Europe, South Africa and Asia
by TBS Ltd, TBS Distribution Centre, Colchester Road,
Frating Green, Colchester CO7 7DW

This edition published in Australia in 2009
by Allen & Unwin Pty Ltd,
PO Box 8500, 83 Alexander Street,
Crows Nest, NSW 2065

Distributed in Canada by
Penguin Books Canada,
90 Eglinton Avenue East, Suite 700,
Toronto, Ontario M4P 2YE

ISBN: 978-190685-004-3

Typeset and designed by Corinthian

Printed and bound in the UK by MPG Books Ltd

CONTENTS

INTRODUCTION

Accepting this commission was at once hard to resist and very unwise. It is one thing to try to please some of the people some of the time. To annoy all of them some of the time is probably foolish, even for a broadcaster, for whom 'one who irritates people by words or mannerisms' might almost be a definition.

The selection that follows will, I am afraid, inevitably offend some. It was a challenge to be asked, however, and a pleasure to sift the rich assortment presented by the game's long history, even if it felt a little like choosing between the peppermint and strawberry creams in an irresistible box of hand-made chocolates.

How do you compare the worth of bowlers, batsmen, wicket-keepers and all-rounders? How can you evaluate men of different eras playing differing amounts of cricket on different pitches with different equipment under different laws? You cannot, and nor can a computer, because no matter what the parameters, a machine cannot assess human qualities: the character, style and aesthetic appeal of a cricketer, all things which have to be part of the equation.

The hardest aspect of this sort of exercise, of course, is judging between those one has seen playing and those about whom one has only read. To take one relatively obscure example, Sri Lankans who saw him still revere the memory of Mahedevan Sathasivam, who 'used his bat like a wand'. He was a heró before his country began to participate in Test cricket and, incidentally, moved to Malaysia having been falsely accused of murdering his wife. Frank Worrell was quoted as saying that 'Sathi' was the best batsman in the world, but he had no chance to prove it on a major stage.

The same is true, alas, of Vintcent Van Der Bijl, the giant but genial South African who was not allowed to play in Test cricket because of the political sins of his country's government when he was causing havoc in domestic cricket. One season for Middlesex in 1980 in which he took 85 Championship wickets at 14 each, and a first-class record of 767 wickets at 16.54, suggest that he could have been another Ken Farnes (who at six foot five was three inches shorter) or even better. Black and 'coloured' South African cricketers before the end of apartheid were, of course, even more sadly destined to waste their sweetness on the desert air. No doubt there were many others whose fame remained largely local because of the social conventions of their time, such as the Indian left-arm spinner Palwankar Baloo, who took more than 100 wickets on tour in England in 1911.

I made two early decisions in compiling this list: to stick both to men's cricket and to Test cricketers, so I have not attempted to consider players before the dawn of official international cricket in 1877. Thus there is no Alfred Mynn, John Small, Billy Beldham, David Harris, William Clarke, Fuller Pilch or John Wisden. Would that this had proved the end of my problems, however!

It is a somewhat chastening thought for me that I have been alive for not far short of half of the 132 years since Test cricket started. Human nature tends to err towards those of whom one has had personal experience and that is no doubt the case here, but so far as natural frailties allow I have tried to be fair and objective in choosing between ancients and moderns, fast bowlers and slow, the pioneers from England and Australia and the one-day champions of today who hail in so many cases from the Indian subcontinent.

The sheer volume of contemporary professional cricket and the availability of a variety of statistics both add to the difficulty. The main criteria, however, have been character, class, temperament, the ability to entertain and the capacity, above all, to win matches by personal performance in a team cause.

Every honest critic has always known that selection is a thankless privilege. Among those I have left out are the pioneering wrist spinners B.J.T. Bosanquet and Bert Vogler; all-rounders as exalted as A.G. Steel, Monty Noble, George Giffen, Frank Foster, George Hirst, Aubrey Faulkner, Alan Davidson, Trevor Bailey, John Reid, Bobby Simpson, Basil D'Oliveira, Mike Procter, Mushtaq Mohammad, Tony Greig and Carl Hooper; and a host of devastating fast bowlers, including the Philadelphian John Barton King, Tom Richardson, Bill

Lockwood, Ted McDonald, Fazal Mahmood, Frank Tyson, Neil Adcock, Peter Heine, Wes Hall, Charlie Griffith, Graeme McKenzie, Peter Pollock, Bob Willis, Jeff Thomson, Joel Garner, Andy Roberts, Craig McDermott, Darren Gough, Andy Caddick, Heath Streak, Brett Lee, Steve Harmison, Makhaya Ntini, Shane Bond and rising forces such as Mitchell Johnson, Lasith Malinga and Ishant Sharma.

Also omitted from the final 100 are many batsmen of imperishable fame, including Clem Hill, A.C. MacLaren, Johnny Tyldesley, R.E. Foster, H.L. Collins, Billy Woodfull, Stan McCabe, Archie Jackson, K.S. Duleepsinhji, Percy Chapman, Bob Wyatt, Herbie Taylor, Bruce Mitchell, Vijay Hazare, Dudley Nourse, Arthur Morris, Sid Barnes, Lindsay Hassett, Bert Sutcliffe, Hanif Mohammad, Rohan Kanhai, Ian Chappell, Majid Khan, Lawrence Rowe, Dilip Vengsarkar, Lala and Mohinder Amarnath, Martin Crowe, Ken McEwan, Robin Smith, Mark Waugh, Aravinda de Silva, Mark Taylor, Mohammad Azharuddin, Michael Slater, Damien Martyn, Justin Langer, Graham Thorpe, Inzamam-ul-Haq, Michael Vaughan, Gary Kirsten, Mohammad Yousuf, Younis Khan, Sourav Ganguly, V.V.S. Laxman, Matthew Hayden, Virender Sehwag, Michael Hussey, Chris Gayle and Shivnarine Chanderpaul. The hardest task of all, perhaps, was to judge current players like Kevin Pietersen against the rest.

Truly it was hard to leave out each one of those I have mentioned. Even the list above does not include twelve batsmen who made more than 100 hundreds – Ernest Tyldesley, Tom Hayward, Phil Mead, Patsy Hendren, Andrew Sandham, Tom Graveney, John Edrich, Glenn Turner, Dennis Amiss, Graeme Hick and Mark Ramprakash.

Then there are the finger spinners Hugh Trumble, Colin Blythe, Sonny Ramadhin, Alf Valentine, Hugh Tayfield, Bob Appleyard, Tony Lock, Johnny Wardle, Derek Underwood, Erapalli Prasanna, Harbhajan Singh, Daniel Vettori and many others; further leg-break and googly merchants of high quality such as Subash Gupte, Stuart MacGill; and wicket-keepers as sparklingly good as Bert Oldfield, Jock Cameron, Don Tallon, Godfrey Evans, Farokh Engineer, Rodney Marsh, Bob Taylor, Wasim Bari, Jeff Dujon, Alec Stewart, Mark Boucher and Brendon McCullum.

I blush at these omissions. Many, I know, will amount to heresy in some quarters. There are several more I could mention. But where do you start and where do you stop? What is a 'great' player? Is he one touched by genius, whether completely fulfilled or not? Is he one who has achieved great things? Must he have courage as well as exceptional talent, and the hard-learned qualities of discipline and patience that successful cricket demands? All who follow certainly have great success in common, but all, too, have something else, that special element that sometimes makes both spectators and fellow players catch their breath in awe.

I wish this book could have been the 200 greatest. Alternatively, had it been a list of personal favourites it would have been very different. I would have started with Graveney, my boyhood hero, and certainly included both the loveably zany Derek Randall and the impish Lindsay Hassett, who was from the top drawer both as a batsman and as a man and always kept cricket in proper perspective. But that would have been quite a different exercise. For this privileged attempt to sort the wheat from the wheat – there is no chaff among the names above – all subjectivity had to be forgotten and lonely decisions had to be made.

Being a selector is a little like being a politician, an invitation to be ridiculed; or, perhaps, like going out to bat against Dennis Lillee on a drying pitch such as the one at Melbourne in 1977. But the umpires are out and the moment has come. Into the breach, dear friends.

THE TOP 100
CRICKETERS
OF ALL TIME

100. C.G. MACARTNEY

Charles George Macartney, b. 27 June 1886, West Maitland, New South Wales; d. 9 September 1958, Sydney

First-class: 15,019 runs (45.78), 419 wickets (20.96) and 102 catches
Tests (35): 2,131 runs (41.78) 45 wickets (27.55) and 17 catches

Ken Hutchings of Kent and England dubbed Charlie Macartney the 'Governor General'. He was short and strong, with broad shoulders and brawny forearms. A calculated risk-taker, not even Don Bradman could dominate an attack more ruthlessly. A better comparison might be with the modern New Zealand swashbuckler Brendon McCullum, but Macartney was far more consistent. He was a tough little right-handed aggressor who batted in Test matches much as opening batsmen now approach the early overs of a Twenty20 or one-day international.

According to Jack Fingleton, Macartney, who was always confident, even cocky, once joked that it was always good policy to aim the first shot at the head of the bowler: 'They don't like it. It rattles them and then you can do as you like.'

Taught the game in an orchard with apples for balls and a tiny bat hand-made by his maternal grandfather, George Moore, who had also played for New South Wales, Macartney was still playing serious cricket when nearly 50 for Frank Tarrant's touring team in India. Eight years previously, aged 40, he had become the second Australian after Victor Trumper to score a century before lunch on the first morning of a Test. Dropped before he had scored in the third Test at Headingley, he made a rapacious 151, baffling the England captain A.W. Carr by his ability to hit balls pitched in the same place to several different places. The modern cricketer would no doubt say that he had 'good angles and great hands'.

This display – he reached his hundred in 103 minutes – was the middle one of his three centuries in successive Tests, following 133 not out at Lord's and preceding another commanding innings of 109 at Old Trafford. Yet on the first of his four tours of England either side of the First World War he had excelled mainly as a remorselessly accurate bowler, slow left-arm after a longish run like the one later employed by Derek Underwood. He had a lethal quicker ball, helping him to take 64 wickets at seventeen on the 1909 tour, including returns of seven for 58 and four for 27 at Leeds.

He dominated in grade cricket for the infant Gordon club and attracted the attention of Monty Noble, making his first Test appearances as an all-rounder in the 1907-08 Ashes series. He served in France for the AIF during the war, winning a Meritorious Service medal for gallantry.

99. VINOO MANKAD

Mulvantrai Himmatial Mankad, b. 12 April 1917, Jamnagar; d. 21 August 1978, Bombay

First-class: 11,591 runs (34.70), 782 wickets (24.53) and 190 catches
Tests (44): 2,109 runs (31.47), 162 wickets (32.32) and 33 catches

Playing as he did in an era when Indian cricket was far less high-profile than it is now, Vinoo Mankad's wider fame rested mainly on his exceptional performances abroad. His extraordinary all-round effort at Lord's on the second of his tours to England in 1952, when he played only in the Tests because of his commitment to the Lancashire League club Haslingden, brought him close to an apotheosis. On the field for twenty hours of a match that occupied just under 25 hours of playing time, he scored 72 and 184 and bowled 97 overs, taking five for 231.

Had it not been for the war his eventual Test figures would have been even more impressive than they are. Until Ian Botham reached the double of 1,000 runs and 100 wickets in 21 Tests, however, Mankad, who did so in 23 games, held a record that not even the likes of Sobers and Miller could match.

Vinoo was a school nickname that stuck – conveniently, no doubt, for cricket reporters. Stocky and smart, with carefully groomed hair, he was a fine fielder and a clever, accurate slow left-arm bowler who hustled through an over in about a minute, with a short run-up and slightly round-arm action. His length and line were invariably immaculate. His batting was demonstrably sound and patient but always attuned to the needs of the side, whether he was opening or batting down the order. He scored mainly in cover drives, late cuts and wristy hits to leg.

He was coached as a young man by the Sussex professional A.F. Wensley and showed his ability against Lionel Tennyson's touring team in 1937-38, when as a twenty-year-old he scored 376 runs at 62 and took fifteen wickets at only fourteen runs each in the unofficial Tests. In 1946 in England he did the double, the only Indian tourist ever to do so, scoring 1,120 runs and taking 129 wickets at twenty. In Australia in 1947-48 his collection was 889 runs and 61 wickets. Although he was upstaged as a batsman in the Tests by Vijay Hazare and mastered by Bradman and Lindwall, he still made 116 and 111 in the two Tests at Melbourne.

Mankad played on for a wide variety of clubs and one of his sons, Ashok, also played Test cricket for India.

98. GORDON GREENIDGE

Gordon Cuthbert Greenidge, b. 1 May 1951, St Peter, Barbados

First-class: 37,354 runs (45.88), 18 wickets (26.61) and 516 catches
Tests (108): 7,558 runs (44.72) and 96 catches

Gordon Greenidge was a pocket Hercules in the tradition of George Headley and Everton Weekes. He was less consistent than either but thrilling to watch, and a match-winner with the same aggressive approach as another Barbadian who opened for Hampshire, Roy Marshall.

A character who seldom seemed at ease with himself off the field, he was the son of Bajan parents who came to live in Reading when he was fourteen. He played for England's under-sixteen team and signed for Hampshire a year later in 1968. Encouraged by Ray Illingworth, the England selectors in 1972 made one of their frequent bids to claim a player who had been moulded overseas, but Greenidge's heart lay in Barbados. He resisted the temptation and in 1974, after two seasons playing for Barbados, he began a Test career for one of the most successful teams in history, going on to score nineteen hundreds in his 108 games.

A brilliant slip fielder and a compact, utterly correct technical batsman, with all the renowned orthodox style of the best West Indians, Greenidge hit the ball incredibly hard, both square of the wicket with resounding hooks and square-cuts, and straight or through the covers off the front foot, never hesitating to hit in the air if necessary. Goodness knows at what pace he might have scored in Twenty20 cricket. As it was he twice hit thirteen sixes in an innings, the first time against the 1974 Pakistan team in England, when he scored 273 in under five hours for an invitation XI at Eastbourne.

As a young man he was occasionally reckless, perhaps in reaction to the polished mastery of his opening partner for Hampshire, Barry

Richards. As he matured, however, so his batting gained discretion. Thereafter, with a stern approach that nicely complemented his less intense, more passionate opening partner Desmond Haynes, he launched many a Test and one-day international innings with panache.

Greenidge and Haynes shared sixteen opening partnerships of more than 100 in 89 Tests together. Their highest was the vengeful 298 against England at Antigua which virtually settled a series that at one stage the West Indies had looked like losing. In fact many of his greatest innings were against England, notably a century in each innings in by no means comfortable conditions at Old Trafford in 1976, and a breathtaking 214 not out off 242 balls with 29 fours and two sixes to win the 1984 Lord's Test against the clock.

Only against Australia was he inconsistent until in 1988-89 he scored 104 at Adelaide and then, with a last flourish, 226 at Bridgetown in 1990-91.

If there was ever a better combination than Greenidge and Haynes (with Viv Richards to follow), Hampshire folk will say it was Greenidge and the other Richards. Their first combination on the old ground at Southampton was worth 201. Greenidge's later contributions included 259 against Sussex in 1975; two hundreds in the match against Kent in 1978, the second of them 120 scored in 91 minutes; and spectacular innings in the one-day tournaments that included 177 in a Gillette Cup match against Glamorgan. His fast bowling son Carl, born in Basingstoke, has also played county cricket.

97. SHAUN POLLOCK

Shaun Maclean Pollock, b. 16 July 1973, Port Elizabeth

First-class: 7,021 runs (33.11), 667 wickets (23.25) and 132 catches
Tests (108): 3,781 runs (32.32), 421 wickets (23.12) and 72 catches

One-day internationals (303): 3,519 runs (26.40), 393 wickets (24.51) and 108 catches

God-fearing and exemplary in his behaviour throughout a long career as one of South Africa's two most reliable all-round cricketers, Shaun Pollock eventually surpassed the achievements both of his fast bowling father Peter and his legendary uncle Graeme.

The fraternal stars of South Africa's brilliant team in the years before their isolation for political reasons hailed from Port Elizabeth, but Shaun was brought up in Durban, Natal. He was never happier than the times when he could return there to recuperate from the remorseless demands of the modern international circuit, but the realities of South Africa's relative lack of prosperity led him to play county cricket for Warwickshire and Durham, and in the fledgling Indian Premier League to boost his earnings.

Tall, red-headed, slim, fit and dedicated, he was a fast bowler with a classical action and a mean bouncer who, guided by the great Barbadian bowler Malcolm Marshall, learned to control the swing and cut of the ball. This helped him greatly in his later years to compensate for a downturn in pace. An athletic, unfailingly reliable fielder, he was also a stylish right-handed batsman who used his full reach to drive and who looked capable of a higher place than the number eight in the order that he most often occupied for his country. In one-day internationals he had an exceptional strike rate of 85.

To an extent the patient Pollock was ground down by his schedule, yet his Test figures are an extraordinary testament to his skill, consistency and stamina. All he lacked when compared to other great all-rounders was the explosiveness of the likes of Keith Miller, Imran Khan and Ian Botham; or, among his contemporaries, Wasim Akram. His superb control and accuracy made him even more of a match-winner in one-day cricket than in Tests. He conceded runs in more than 300 internationals at the miserly rate of 3.68 – in Tests it was 2.39 – and the only real blemish was his relative failure as a captain in the wake of Hansie Cronje's shocking fall from grace in 2000. In particular Pollock, whose integrity, unlike his predecessor's, was transparent, misunderstood a technicality in the rules that resulted in South Africa's elimination from the first World Cup to be held on their own grounds in 2003. But his human qualities shone away from home, not least when his own century in Bridgetown helped to win the series in 2000-01.

The majority of his wickets were earned through niggling away on or around the off stump, invariably on a good length and often getting extra bounce or movement off the seam. He scored two Test centuries and took five wickets in an innings sixteen times, but any captain knew he could be relied upon to slow the other side's scoring rate. To him sometimes should have gone much of the credit for many of the wickets earned through the greater hostility of his two main partners, Allan Donald and Makhaya Ntini.

Despite his genes it was Marshall, who joined Natal a year after Pollock's debut in 1992-93, who became a greater mentor than his own fast-bowling father. The pupil was ready for Test cricket by 1995, taking five for 32 in England's second innings in the decisive final Test at Newlands to seal a home win. Against Pakistan in Faisalabad in 1997 he took five for 37 to help bowl out Pakistan for 92 when they needed only 146 to win the deciding Test. Three months later came perhaps his greatest performance, seven for 87 against Australia from 41 overs in hot weather at Adelaide. As captain he also took ten wickets in the match against India at Bloemfontain in 2001-02.

96. VIJAY MERCHANT

Vijay Madhavji Thackersey Merchant, b. 12 October 1911, Bombay; d. 27 October 1987, Bombay

First-class: 13, 470 runs (71.64), 65 wickets (32.12) and 115 catches
Tests (10): 859 runs (47.72) and seven catches

India's first great Test batsman, Vijay Merchant averaged 71 in first-class cricket, second only to Bradman. He played so little cricket by

modern standards that evaluating him against a present-day master such as V.V.S. Laxman, other very consistent and high-class batsmen like Dilip Vengsarkar and Mohinder Amarnath or the mercurial genius Mohammad Azharuddin is impossible. But Merchant succeeded against the best when the opportunities came, so there can be no denying his exceptional quality.

He obviously loved batting and there were suggestions late in his career that rivalry from Vijay Hazare caused the two of them to put occupation of the crease ahead of the needs of their team. That was not, however, typical of Merchant, nor unknown in cricket teams in India or anywhere else. The fact is that he was a masterful little batsman with quick footwork, a brilliant cutter either square or late, adept off his legs, quick to spot the ball to hook and a crisp driver when it was pitched up. Discretion, however, was the key to his success.

At the age of fifteen he had seen C.K. Nayadu strike MCC for eleven sixes and thirteen fours in his 153 for the Hindus. From a wealthy family in Bombay, his family name was Thackersey, but at school in Bombay his Parsee headmaster gave him the name Merchant after the boy apparently thought he was being asked for his father's profession.

A forerunner to the likes of Hanif Mohammad and Geoff Boycott, his approach to batting was studious and thorough. Before his first visit to England in 1936 he prepared by batting on dew-covered grass in the early mornings, and when he arrived he asked Jack Hobbs to assess his technique in the nets. Not previously an opening batsman, he was asked to become one on the tour and responded by sharing an opening partnership of 203 with the more eye-catching Mushtaq Ali in the Old Trafford Test.

In a wet summer Merchant scored 1,745 runs at 51. When he got home, while others who had toured England were exhausted by playing so much more cricket than they were used to, he played in four Ranji Trophy matches and scored a century in each of them.

He did even better on his second tour of England in 1946 when, despite more damp pitches, he scored 2,385 runs at 74.53, including double centuries against Lancashire and Sussex and a century in the Oval Test. His overall average in the Ranji trophy was 98 and he scored sixteen centuries from only 47 innings. Ill health prevented his going on the post-war tours to Australia and the West Indies, and a bad shoulder injury sustained when he dived for a ball in the field after scoring 151 against England at Delhi in 1951-52 ended his career, but he became an influential cricket commentator and administrator.

95. C.T.B. TURNER

Charles Thomas Biass Turner, b. 16 November 1862, Bathurst, New South Wales; d. Manly, Sydney, 1 January 1944

First-class: 3,856 runs (15.54) and 993 wickets (14.24)
Tests (17): 323 runs (11.53) and 101 wickets (16.53)

Both his epithet – 'The Terror' – and his extraordinary bowling fig-ures tell the story of Charlie Turner, who formed Australia's first great opening bowling partnership with the left-armed Jack Ferris. In 1888, when their alliance was at its most extraordinary in England, he took 314 wickets on the tour at 11.12. Between them he and Ferris took 534 of the 663 wickets, devastating opposition of mixed quality, often on rain-affected pitches, and bowling unchanged on twenty occasions. In the first-class games Turner's haul was 283 wickets at 11.68 apiece. Yet England won a low scoring Test series 2-1.

It was skill rather than extreme speed that gave Turner his fear-some reputation. He had what was described as a graceful, springy approach to the stumps and was once timed, at Woolwich, as bowling at no more than 55 mph. Modern technology apparently recorded a ball from Shoaib Akhtar in the 2003 World Cup at 100 mph, to which the ghost of Turner might well respond: 'look at the scorebook'. Pitches were different, batting techniques different and so, for that matter, were the methods used to measure speed. That he was timed at all suggests that he was reckoned to be pretty quick.

Turner was sturdy but of no more than medium height. Photographs show him sometimes with a moustache; sometimes, unusually for the period, without. Using fingers and wrist he would cut the ball back sharply from the off, starting with an open-chested action. In one game alone against an England eleven at Hastings he took seventeen wickets for 50, fourteen of them bowled and two LBW. That could only signify phenomenal accuracy.

The son of an English innkeeper who had emigrated twenty years before Turner's birth, he did not even make the first eleven at Bathurst Grammar School in Sydney, but assiduous practice at the local cricket club paid off. He made his name almost overnight when he took seventeen wickets for XXII of Bathurst against the touring English team in 1881-82, including all ten in the second innings.

He played for New South Wales from the following season but, perhaps because of his odd action, it took him four seasons to establish a regular place. At last in 1886-87 he was selected for Australia after taking eight for 32 and six for 27 against the latest England touring team, and he immediately repeated his success with six for fifteen to rout England, in company with Ferris, for 45 in his first Test in Sydney. Nine for 93 followed in the next match and by the end of that season he had become the first Australian to take more than 100 wickets in a domestic season.

He toured England three times, taking 148 wickets on the third visit in 1893. Later he set himself up as a stockbroker in Queensland and received two public testimonials before retiring to his home city of Sydney.

94. BHAGWAT CHANDRASEKHAR

Bhagwat Subramanya Chandrasekhar, b. 17 May 1945, Mysore

First-class: 600 runs (4.61), 1,063 wickets (24.04) and 107 catches
Tests (58): 167 runs (4.07), 242 wickets (29.74) and 25 catches

Amid India's rich tradition of classical spin bowlers Bhagwat Chandrasekhar stands out as something quite different. He was primarily a topspin and googly bowler with a brisk, straight approach to the crease after holding the ball in front of his face at the start of his run-up, like a golfer memorising the line of his shot. There followed a swift turn of a right arm that was withered by polio in his youth, but seldom has a disability been put to better use.

His arm would come so straight past his head that he seemed in danger of removing his right ear, his stock ball either skidding through straight or turning a little from leg. He had to throw with his left arm and he was a natural number eleven, whose highest first-class score, 25, was a triumph.

While everything else seemed to happen almost in slow motion around him when he was bowling, including the graceful motion of his chief partner Bishen Singh Bedi, 'Chandra' (admittedly supported by his keen wicket-keeping accomplices Farokh Engineer and Syed Kirmani) was all action and urgency.

With Bedi and two high-class off-spinners, Erapally Prasanna and Srinisvasaraghavan Venkataraghavan, he was the means of India's many successes, mainly under the leadership of Ajit Wadekar, in the early 1970s. Chandra was the most dangerous of the famous four, especially on a wearing pitch when his bowling, with at least two short-legs waiting for edges off his high-bouncing googly, had a snake-like venom.

Nor was he merely a force to be reckoned with at home. At the Oval in 1971 his six for 38 hounded England to defeat, their first in a series at home against India. In the New Year Test against Australia in 1978 he took twelve wickets for 104 at Melbourne to enable India to beat Australia for the first time away. They were the best figures by any Indian bowler in Australia and enabled Chandra to become only the second, and by three matches the quickest, Indian bowler to take 200 Test wickets, in his 48th game.

His peak performance was his haul of 35 wickets in five Tests at home to England in 1972-73, when his wickets came at only eighteen runs each. Normally he traded some full tosses and long-hops, but no batsman could ever rest against this amiable South Indian.

He had made an immediate impact in Test cricket, taking four for

67 at the Brabourne Stadium, Bombay, against Mike Smith's England team when he was only eighteen. Three of his victims, typically, were bowled, surprised by nip off the pitch. On the same ground against Australia nine months later he claimed eight batsmen, of whom four were bowled and two LBW. Gradually opponents learned that it was safer to get well forward to him, but with close fielders at hand it was not often a comfortable policy.

93. GRAEME SMITH

Graeme Craig Smith, b. 1 February 1981, Johannesburg

First-class: 9,291 runs (50.77), eleven wickets (95.27) and 157 catches
Tests (76): 6,340 runs (50.31), eight wickets (100.12) and 102 catches
One-day internationals (136): 5,111 runs (40.88), eighteen wickets (52.83) and 72 catches

Graeme Smith did not quite look like a great player, even when he was churning out successive double hundreds in his first two Tests in England at the tender age of 22. Tenderness and Smith were, in fact, uneasy bedfellows: he was already hard enough to spend any night on a bed of nails. Only nine when Nelson Mandela was released from captivity, he grew up believing in a multiracial society and the fruits of hard work.

Mature far beyond his years, he continued to prove his capacity for learning under pressure, to the extent that he became a batsman who could almost be guaranteed to succeed when it most mattered. No less to his credit, he has become one of the game's great leaders, rising above difficult issues of selection in an era when South Africa was trying to promote as many black and 'coloured' cricketers as reasonably possible in line with government policy. Often abrasive,

and seldom much liked by opponents, he followed Ian Chappell's dictum that captaincy is not a popularity contest. Instead he demanded respect and got it.

Not for Smith captaining from mid-off in the traditional way. He sees everything from first slip, where he catches anything above ground in huge hands, like a dolphin swallowing fish. Presenting his considerable bulk to the bowler at the start of every South African innings, whatever the duration of the game, he radiates self-belief. His footwork is decisive, if a little heavy, which has rendered him vulnerable to bowlers swinging the ball into his pads with a new ball, notably Matthew Hoggard in 2004-05. But he drives powerfully, picks up runs deftly off his legs and has become a fine player of spin. More than 10,000 international runs before his 28th birthday left little doubt about his skill and none about his character.

Two England captains have wilted and fallen in the face of his iron will. An innings of 187 in his first first-class match, ten Test caps and a double hundred were already on his CV before his first series in charge in 2003. Success came at once. His two innings at Edgbaston, 277 and 85 from 70 balls, hastened Nasser Hussain's resignation.

Hussain's successor, Michael Vaughan, lost his first Test as captain thanks to Smith's follow-up, a flawless and remorseless 259 at Lord's. Five crowded years later, Vaughan himself resigned after Smith had scored 154 not out on a turning pitch to win the Edgbaston Test by five wickets. South Africa went on to beat England away for the first time since their reinstatement to international cricket after the dismantling of apartheid in 1991.

There were inevitable setbacks after his glorious start but further triumphs too. At the Wanderers stadium in his native Johannesburg Australia hammered his bowlers for a record 434 for four. Smith responded with 90 from 55 balls and an opening partnership of 187 in 20.1 overs, with the still more gifted, but erratic, Herschelle Gibbs. South Africa, against all odds, won with a ball to spare. Then, at Perth late in 2008, he ignored pain from an elbow injury to set his side the perfect example, striking a bold hundred as South Africa chased 414 to beat Australia by six wickets, the second highest fourth-innings run chase in Test history. The jut of his jaw was never more prominent and South Africa went on to claim the series.

92. COURTNEY WALSH

Courtney Andrew Walsh, b. 30 October 1962, Kingston, Jamaica

First-class: 4,530 runs (11.32), 1807 wickets (21.71) and 117 catches
Tests (132): 936 runs (7.54), 519 wickets (24.44) and 29 catches
One-day internationals (205): 321 runs (6.97), 227 wickets (30.47) and
27 catches

West Indians, generally speaking, have shown more dignity in the face of triumph or disaster than any of the other 'nationalities' in the age of widely televised international cricket. Courtney Walsh, a proud Jamaican, straddled (with immensely long legs) the period between the era of West Indian domination of world cricket and the time when the long supply line of fast bowlers came to an abrupt halt. He treated the two impostors just the same.

Walsh, all his life a loyal member of the Melbourne Club in Kingston from which Michael Holding also emanated, became the Duracell of world cricket. Immensely strong and tall, with a back as straight as the trunk of a mahogany, he bowled more than 30,000 balls for the West Indies in 132 Tests, retiring with a record number of 519 wickets, over 100 more than any previous bowler from the Caribbean. Like Tom Richardson in the early days of professional cricket for Surrey and England, he would bowl until he dropped.

In Walsh's case a Test series had barely finished, it seemed, before a one-day series began. He bowled another 21,881 balls in one-day cricket overall for a return of 551 wickets, taken at an average cost of 25 runs each. He got a wicket in one-day cricket every 40 balls on average and conceded fewer than four runs per over (3.79), despite one memorable mauling by Allan Lamb in a World Cup match at Gujranwala in 1987, when he conceded 31 runs in two overs. It was typical of Walsh that he learned from the experience.

He had already broadened his horizons by joining Gloucestershire

in 1984, having been recommended by Tom Graveney. He arrived after they had finished bottom in the Championship. In his first two seasons they came third and second and he took 203 wickets, changing his pace cleverly but never stinting himself nor bowling with anything less than sustained hostility. 'He is a marvellous team man,' said his captain David Graveney. 'Courtney has the knack of defusing awkward situations with a humorous remark or some genial clowning.'

In 1986 he took 118 Championship wickets for Gloucestershire at 18.17, taking five or more wickets in an innings eleven times, and nine for 72 against Somerset. He played for the county when he could until 1998, captaining them for three seasons. Such was the depth of his character that in time he also led both Jamaica and the West Indies.

At just under six foot six inches, he had a long run. His action was open-chested but high. It stood up to the demands of a total of 85, 443 balls in first-class cricket alone. Most of his wickets were the result of extra bounce, or hitting the seam with the ball angled in to the right-handed batsman only for it to straighten and take an outside edge.

Often the journeyman in his early days in the West Indies side, and overshadowed to an extent by the likes of Roberts, Holding and Marshall, he became the mainspring, sharing a formidable new-ball attack with Curtly Ambrose. As captain in India in 1994, he told his team before the last Test in Chandigarh, with his side one down in the rubber, that he had never played in a losing series for the West Indies. In fact they had gone 27 matches without defeat. He took only five wickets in the match, but his side won by 243 runs.

Soon after, Walsh took seven for 37 and six for eighteen on a juicy pitch at Wellington, where his side beat New Zealand by an innings and 322 runs.

During the last five years of a career that lasted until 2000-01 such triumphs were few and far between, but his cool demeanour and hooded eyes revealed none of his inner pain.

91. IAN HEALY

Ian Healy, b. 30 April 1964, Brisbane

First-class: 8,341 runs (30.22), 698 catches, 69 stumpings
Tests (119): 4,356 runs (27.39), 366 catches and 29 stumpings

A genial enough character with a beer in hand, Ian Healey was a cricketer of rare tenacity, with keen eyes and wiry red hair like a fox terrier. He was a neat, agile, courageous wicket-keeper in the tradition of Bert Oldfield, Don Tallon, Wally Grout and Rodney Marsh, and one of the hardiest of a hardy breed. By virtue of willpower, a forceful personality and relentless practice, he became perhaps the best pure wicket-keeping technician of them all.

Although he was not as good a batsman as Marsh nor remotely as brilliant as his successor for Australia, Adam Gilchrist, his performances in the late middle order were never to be underestimated. Four Test hundreds were testament to that.

He set the standard of Australian professionalism in his era, so much so that the term 'work ethic' became commonplace when he was discussed. He would get up at dawn to practise against a wall with a golf ball and just a pair of inner gloves, often in the basement car park of the team's hotel.

Picked for Australia after only six first-class games for Queensland, all of them as a substitute for the established keeper, he struggled initially on the low-bouncing pitches of Queensland, but in England in 1993 he broke through with a vengeance. Not only did he make his maiden first-class hundred off 133 balls in a bold attacking innings at Old Trafford but he dismissed 26 batsmen in the five Tests, 21 caught and five stumped off Shane Warne, with whom he soon established a rapport that overwhelmed many opposing batsmen.

With Warne groaning and gesticulating from one end and Healy chuntering constantly at the other, there was no respite. Both

pushed gamesmanship close to the limit of acceptability within the game's spirit. But Healy was outwitted one day at Sydney when Mike Atherton survived an edge into the wicket-keeper's gloves, unnoticed by the umpire. Healy never stopped sledging the thick-skinned Lancastrian until he reached his only Test hundred in Australia, whereupon he warmly congratulated him before saying: 'Why didn't you walk, you Pommy bastard.' Atherton simply replied: 'When in Rome ...' which silenced his opponent for several overs before he returned, apparently bemused, to the subject. 'We're not in Rome, mate. We're in bloody Sydney.'

Wherever he was, Healy competed with zeal and rare consistency, never more determined than in an Ashes series. Dropped off a skier at the Gabba in the first Test of the 1998-99 series he scored a swash-buckling 134, rubbing salt into the wounds with an almost visible glee. His highest innings, 161 not out, was also played at the Gabba when Australia were in trouble against the West Indies. But it is as a wicket-keeper of rare poise and polish that he will be remembered.

90. LANCE GIBBS

Lancelot Richard Gibbs, b. 29 September 1934, Georgetown, Guyana

First-class: 1,729 runs (8.55), 1,024 wickets (27.22) and 203 catches
Tests (79): 488 runs (6.97), 309 wickets (29.09) and 52 catches

Lance Gibbs was a thin and sinewy off-spinner with long fingers who, with a very short run-up and a swift right arm which flighted the ball higher than any bowler since, could never have prospered in contemporary cricket as he did in his heyday. Not by bowling in the same way, at least. Heavy bats, shorter boundaries and stronger, fitter batsmen would have forced him to offer less temptation. But he was a master of his art, and few bowlers have twirled the ball so frequently above the batsman's eye-line. From there it would descend to bounce as well as to turn, often via bat or glove into the waiting hands of his favourite short-leg fieldsman, Garfield Sobers.

Gibbs retired just before the West Indies discovered, under the leadership of his cousin and fellow countryman Clive Lloyd, an almost infallible method of winning – and not losing – Test matches, namely by using fast bowlers for most of the day. Gibbs belonged to a more balanced era, plying his trade at home for Guyana and the West Indies, and in England for Warwickshire, for whom his beguiling flight worked wonders. Although he was a mature bowler by the time that he arrived at Edgbaston to qualify for a year in 1967 he became, like many a West Indian, a much wiser professional for his experience in county cricket. In particular he was encouraged by his captain, M.J.K. Smith, to bowl more often from round the wicket, especially when the ball was turning sharply. In 1971, at the age of 36, he bowled more than a thousand first-class overs for Warwickshire, taking 131 wickets at 18.89.

Learning his game initially at the Demerara Cricket Club in Georgetown where Lloyd and Roy Fredericks also played, he first appeared for British Guiana beside the 1954-5 MCC touring team, dismissing Denis Compton and, for 231, Tom Graveney. Initially he was a leg-spinner who bowled only the occasional off break.

Persistence, guileful changes of pace, great stamina and the character to overcome a sore spinning finger that often became painfully swollen below the knuckle of his index finger, saw him through a long career during which he made four tours of England, three to Australia and India, and one each to New Zealand and Pakistan, where he took seventeen wickets at 23 in four Tests in 1958-59. In Australia in 1960-61 he took nineteen at twenty in three Tests, including three wickets in four balls on the spin-friendly Bulli soil of Sydney. In 1961-62 he had a spell of eight for six in 15.3 overs (eight for 38 overall) in the second innings to win the Bridgetown Test against India. In England, on the memorable 1963 tour, his 78 wickets included 26 at 21 runs each in the Tests.

He retired to the United States and even played for them, as well as managing two West Indies sides, neither of which possessed a spinner of his exalted class.

89. BRIAN STATHAM

John Brian Statham, b. 17 June 1930, Manchester; d. 11 June 2000, London

First-class: 5,424 runs, (10.80) 2,260 wickets (16.37) and 230 catches
Tests (70): 675 runs (11.44), 252 wickets (24.84) and 28 catches

Double joints enabled Brian Statham to take off his sweater in an instant by crossing his hands over his waist as he walked towards the wicket before the start of an over. In his youth he could also wrap both legs around his neck. The same loose effortlessness made him a superb fielder in the deep, and it was the chief characteristic of a bowling action that made him England's most accurate and reliable fast bowler through a long, distinguished career in which about the only thing he ever complained about was sore feet.

Statham, variously known as 'George', 'Greyhound' and 'Whippet', was a gentle, softly spoken, modest Lancastrian who got on with the job and carried on until it was done. He was a complete natural, his run-up and delivery fluid and uncoached. He was also stoically unselfish, leaving any downhill slope or, more importantly, any following wind, to his two great partners Frank Tyson and Fred Trueman.

He appeared from almost nowhere in England (or MCC) colours on the 1950-51 tour of Australia when sent out to reinforce Freddie Brown's injury-stricken team. He was in the selectors' notebooks because of a sensational opening spell in the Roses match the

previous summer, his first in the Lancashire side following national service. In his second game, having just turned twenty, he had taken the first five Somerset wickets for five runs at Bath.

Statham's alliance with Tyson won the Ashes for England under Len Hutton in 1954-55. Tyson was the typhoon, a little wild but frighteningly fast, Statham the one who gave the batsmen no respite at the other end. He took five wickets bowling into a brutal wind from Botany Bay in the Test at Sydney just before Christmas in which Tyson turned the series with six for 85; then five for 60 in the first innings at Melbourne, and another three in the second innings of the fourth Test at Adelaide that settled the series.

His seven for 39 at Lord's in 1955 won a close game against South Africa and he took eleven wickets against the same opposition at Lord's in 1960, exploiting the invisible ridge; but seven for 57 at Melbourne in 1958-59 was not enough to make up for England's batting failure.

Season after season he bowled tirelessly and to the highest standards for Lancashire, taking 1,816 wickets for them. He captained his county from 1965 to 1967, became their president, and was awarded a CBE for his services to the game.

88. ABDUL QADIR

Abdul Qadir Khan, b. 15 September 1955, Lahore

First-class: 3,636 runs (18.74), 897 wickets (23.43) and 83 catches
Tests (38): 1,029 runs (15.59), 236 wickets (32.80) and fifteen catches
One-day internationals (104): 641 runs (15.26), 132 wickets (26.08) and 21 catches

The moment that Abdul Qadir came on to bowl in any match was always one to get a crowd buzzing and the batsmen mentally and

physically on their toes. From the same temperamental mould as Bill O'Reilly, Tony Lock and Shane Warne, Qadir was a slow bowler with a fast man's approach. He expected wickets at once.

Stocky and passionate, he used strong fingers and a supple right wrist to spin his leg-breaks, googlies, two slightly different top spinners and the flipper with exceptional zest. His bounding, exuberant action suggested that he was going to bowl the ball quicker and flatter than he actually did. On the contrary, he had deceptive loop and the fizz and bounce off the pitch, even sometimes on Pakistan's slow, flat pitches, that harried batsmen into error.

He announced himself as a match winner with figures of eight for 29 and four for 86 for Habib Bank against Universities at Lahore in 1977-78, after which he was a certainty to play against the England touring team. He took six for 44 to bowl them out for 191 in the first innings of the second Test at Hyderabad.

His shoulder injury spared England further serious damage during the following home season but in 1982 he was the star of the tour, bamboozling county batsmen to take 57 wickets in twelve games. His return of ten in the three Tests was deceptively modest, but in 1982-83 he became the first Pakistan bowler to take 100 wickets in a domestic season, taking nine wickets in an innings for Habib Bank against both Karachi and Rawalpindi plus 22 Test wickets against the touring Australians.

The following season, his eighteen wickets in three Tests inspired Pakistan to their first series victory against England. He also took fourteen in the West Indies in the tense series in the Caribbean in 1987-88 when Pakistan would have beaten the world champions, had Qadir had more co-operation from the umpires. Always inclined to volatility, he punched a mocking spectator during the Bridgetown Test. In 1985 he had been sent home from New Zealand 'for disciplinary reasons'.

Very effective also as a one-day bowler, he conceded only just over four runs an over (4.05) in his 104 internationals and he was never to be underestimated as a batsman, scoring two first-class hundreds, the first of them in only his second first-class match.

87. NEIL HARVEY

Robert Neil Harvey, b. 8 October 1928, Melbourne

First-class: 21,699 runs (50.93) 30 wickets (36.86) and 229 catches
Tests (79) 6,149 runs (48.41), three wickets (40.00) and 64 catches

Few batsmen, and no younger ones, have started with such a surge of brilliance as Neil Harvey. By the age of 21 he had already scored five Test hundreds. He made 21 in all and 67 in first-class cricket, but his class was never better demonstrated than it was against the harrying fast bowling of Tyson and Statham at Sydney in 1954-55, when Harvey scored 92 not out with quiet mastery in a total of 184 all out.

A neat, trim, dark-haired left-hander with perfect footwork, he always batted without a cap and never had to stretch to play the ball: it was always beneath his nose. The blade of his bat seemed always to meet the ball in the middle, even when he was hitting square of the wicket. Constantly in search of runs – although he could defend in a crisis as a four-and-a-half-hour 69 out of 140 against Jim Laker and Tony Lock at Headingley in 1956 demonstrated – he was something of an antidote to the run gorgers of Australia before the war. Told by a selector that he could have made 300 just after he had been caught for 50 he retorted: 'Whoever wants to make 300?'

One of six brothers, four of whom played first-class cricket, Neil was born after the family had moved to Victoria from Broken Hill in New South Wales where his father had been a miner. In Melbourne the boys learned their cricket playing with a tennis ball on a cobbled lane, sharpening their reactions, before getting more formal training at the Fitzroy Club.

The eldest brother, Mervyn, was already an established batsman for Victoria when Neil, aged only nineteen, made his first hundred for Australia against India. He was the happy young prodigy in Bradman's experienced side of 'Invincibles' in England in 1948,

scoring 112 in his first Ashes Test at Headingley. He mastered Hugh Tayfield with 151 at Durban in 1949-50, and at home in 1952-53 made 834 runs in the five Tests against South Africa, including a scintillating 116 in 106 minutes at Adelaide and 205, his highest Test score, in the fifth Test at Melbourne. It was his eighth century in ten Tests against South Africa. No wonder he married a South African girl.

Apart from four tours of England, on the last of which he stood in for Richie Benaud as captain at Lord's and guided Australia to victory, Harvey toured the West Indies, Pakistan and India, making 204 at Kingston and 96 against Pakistan on the coconut matting at Dacca, where no one else could master Fazal Mahmood. Throughout his career he was a superb cover fielder.

86. ZAHEER ABBAS

Zaheer Abbas, b. 24 July 1947, Sialkot

First-class: 34,843 runs (51.54), 30 wickets (38.20) and 278 catches
Tests (78): 5,062 runs (44.79), three wickets (44.00) and 34 catches

Judged either by figures or by his élan and the pleasure he gave, Zaheer Abbas was a great batsman. He smiled a lot and he delighted in the aesthetic beauty of batting. Tallish, lean and elegant, he batted for most of his career in glasses, switching eventually to contact lenses. Swift to assess the line and length of the ball after a flourishing, semi-circular backlift, and moving easily forwards or backwards, he scored mainly in boundaries, driving with a flowing grace, almost invariably along the ground and on both sides of the wicket.

Only on the green, bouncy pitches that became more common in Australia in the 1970s did he look unhappy, but he still made scores

of 85, 101, 90 and 58 in the first two Tests of Pakistan's 1976-77 tour of Australia, when Dennis Lillee was in his prime.

Having averaged 93 in the Qaid-e-Azam Trophy in 1967, he burst onto the international scene with a wonderful innings of 274 against England at Edgbaston in 1971, in only his second Test match. Batting for more than nine hours, he stroked 38 fours. He scored two more Test double hundreds, at the Oval in 1974 and at Lahore against India in 1978-79, having scored 176 and 96 at Faisalabad in the previous match, the first between Pakistan and India for seventeen years.

It was English crowds and especially Bristol ones who saw the best of him. They called him, simply, 'Z'. He never learned to speak very good English (and his team-mates certainly never learned Urdu) but his stroke play charmed in itself. From 1972 he made more than 1,000 runs in eleven seasons for Gloucestershire, including 2,554 in the hot summer of 1976 when every batsman of quality seemed to prosper.

No one has exceeded Zaheer's feat of scoring a hundred in both innings of a match on eight occasions. Four of these, also a record, included a double century. He did it twice in 1976: 216 not out and 156 not out against Surrey at the Oval, and 230 not out and 104 not out against Kent at Canterbury. Cheltenham and Bath, against Sussex and Somerset, were the scenes of the other two instances. He was the ideal Festival player, an entertainer at home on green fields among the white marquees.

At home in Lahore, in 1982-83, he became the twentieth batsman to reach 100 first-class hundreds, not uncharacteristically going on to a double hundred, against India. Always a man of purple patches, he followed up with hundreds in the next two Tests. Only Bradman, Compton, Hutton and Boycott needed fewer than his 658 innings to post his 100th hundred.

'I hate fielding,' he once said. He was a good fielder, in fact; but he batted as though he was keen to avoid it.

85. MICHAEL HOLDING

Michael Anthony Holding, b. 16 February 1954, Halfway Tree, Kingston, Jamaica

First-class: 3,600 runs (15), 778 wickets (23.43) and 125 catches
Tests (60): 910 runs (13.78), 249 wickets (23.68) and 22 catches
One-day internationals (102): 282 runs (9.10), 142 wickets (21.37) and 30 catches

With a footfall as soft as an impala's and an easy elegance all his own, Michael Holding's fast bowling was like noiseless thunder. Umpires, accustomed to sharpening their senses as a bowler's footsteps approached from behind, said that they could not hear him coming, despite one of the longest run-ups of any great bowler; hence his sobriquet 'Whispering Death'. To the onlooker he seemed to float to the wicket, his arms loose and his head nodding like a newly born baby's.

Still slim, tall and graceful, whether playing cricket or roving the world as a wise, passionate and scrupulously fair commentator for Sky television, with a beguiling bass voice and unchanged Jamaican accent, he has always fought for justice and common sense in cricket. In his youth in Australia he would come close to tears when an umpire turned down a legitimate appeal, and in New Zealand he was so frustrated by a home-town decision by a local umpire that he took a long kick at the stumps like a full-back converting a try, although much more elegantly. In retirement, he resigned from the cricket committee of the International Cricket Council on a point of principle.

He came into the West Indies team just as the policy of blitzing opponents with four fast bowlers was evolving in the late 1970s. As such he was a party not only to some of the worst excesses – intimidation by bouncers, notably at Old Trafford in 1976, and slowed-down over-rates – but also to some of the greatest performances of one of the great teams of history.

Their methods were a reaction to those employed by Ian Chappell's Australians in the mid 1970s when Dennis Lillee and Jeff

Thomson were demoralising opponents with speed, albeit as part of a more balanced attack. Holding was outstanding in England in 1976, taking 55 wickets at fourteen runs each on the tour. On the bone-dry but lifeless pitch at the Oval in August he produced his greatest performance, taking fourteen wickets for 149 simply by bowling fast and straight to a full length.

He played domestic cricket in England, for Derbyshire, and in Australia, for Tasmania, but remained a certain choice whenever he was fit for the West Indies. This was despite all the other top-class fast bowlers available at different times in his career, including Joel Garner, Andy Roberts, Wayne Daniel, Sylvester Clarke, Colin Croft, Malcolm Marshall and Curtly Ambrose. Hunting in packs as they did it was difficult to evaluate them individually, not only against each other or contemporaries who were ploughing lonelier furrows, such as Bob Willis, but against previous standard-bearers such as Learie Constantine and Wes Hall. The fact is that, charming fellow though he was and is in conversation about the day's racing prospects, no opponent would be sorry if Holding happened not to be playing. A hurdler in his youth, with the ability to become one of Jamaica's great athletes, he settled instead for the art of bowling very fast.

84. GILBERT JESSOP

Gilbert Laird Jessop, b. 19 November 1874, Cheltenham; d. 5 November 1955, Fordington, Dorset

First-class: 26,698 runs (32.63), 872 wickets (22.79) and 463 catches
Tests (18): 569 runs (21.880), ten wickets (35.40) and eleven catches

The Croucher, so called because of his low, wide batting stance, like a cat ready to pounce, was a legend even in his playing days. He was a

dangerous fast bowler who twice took 100 wickets in a season, one of the greatest of all cover fielders and, above all, that greatest of crowd-pleasers, a hitter who set out to attack at almost all times. How he would have revelled in Twenty20 cricket, and the limited-overs game generally. Until 1910, late in his career, sixes had to go out of the ground, not just to clear the boundary, yet he hit them frequently in every substantial innings he played.

At the Hastings Festival, his favourite playground, he scored 191 in 1907 between 2.15 pm and 3.45 pm. His 180 scores of 50 or more were scored at an average rate of 79.08 runs an hour, and although his Test record was a disappointment he played perhaps the most famous innings an Englishman ever has, on a wet and brutal Oval pitch in the fifth Test of 1902.

Needing 263 to win the game after Australia had retained the Ashes, England plunged from ten for three to 48 for five. Accompanied first by F.S. Jackson then by George Hirst, Jessop, who was actually reining himself in to avoid being caught deep on the leg-side off one of Hugh Trumble's off-breaks, reached 50 out of 70 in only 43 minutes with a variety of strokes. According to C.B. Fry: 'Jessop then let himself loose like a catapult at the bowling and shattered it to smithereens'. He reached his hundred in 75 minutes. The wild joy at his century from a crowd of 18,000 disturbed his concentration and he was caught behind square-leg for 104, but England won by one wicket thanks to a last wicket partnership of fifteen by Hirst and Wilfred Rhodes.

The Croucher finished with a modest Test record, but good judges like Pelham Warner and A.C. MacLaren felt that he should always be picked for his capacity to turn any game in an hour's batting, not to mention his rapacious fielding. Sammy Woods wrote that he saved 30 runs before even going out to bat. Anonymous verses in the *Athletic News* warned:

When you hit a ball hard and straight to Jessop
Do not run at all, or your stumps he'll mess up.
Swoop! He's got the ball. Whish, it's in the wicket!
Fluke? Oh, not at all – that's Jessopian cricket.

Short but broad, deep-chested and with long arms, he used a much heavier bat than his contemporaries, often one well over three pounds. Mainly a hostile bowler at Cambridge and in early days for Gloucestershire, he scored 55 first-class centuries between 1894 and 1914. Four times he scored a hundred in each innings, yet he was out for scores of between nought and ten in 34 per cent of all his innings, making 70 ducks. As a batsman he lived and died by the sword but as a character he was modest, kind, universally liked and respected.

83. ALLAN DONALD

Allan Anthony Donald, b. 20 October 1966, Bloemfontein

First-class: 2,785 runs (12.85), 1,216 wickets (22.76) and 115 catches
Tests (72), 652 runs (10.69), 330 wickets (22.25) and eighteen catches
One-day internationals (164): 94 runs (4.27) and 272 wickets (21.79)

Allan Donald was one of the essential pillars of South African cricket in the post-apartheid era. By the time his country was welcomed back onto the international circuit, he was already established as a thoroughbred fast bowler with more than 400 first-class wickets. His natural talent might have made him a great Olympic athlete had he not been drawn to cricket. Fair-haired and overtly hostile, he was dubbed 'White Lightning' and he was indeed extremely quick.

His action, honed by Bob Woolmer, his respected coach at Warwickshire and later for South Africa, was a fine example of smoothly gathering force, culminating in a leap, with the eyes aiming levelly at the batsman over his left shoulder before the full swing of a lithe body and long right arm.

He played his first game for the former Orange Free State in 1985, took eight for 37 against Transvaal two seasons later and in 1989, as

Warwickshire's overseas player, 86 wickets at 16.25. In his first international against India at Calcutta in November 1991 he took five for 29, and he was an automatic selection from then until an ankle injury hampered him late in his career. He carried South Africa to their first Test victory of the new era with twelve for 139 against India at Port Elizabeth in 1992-93, taking seven for 84 in the second innings.

He topped the English bowling averages again in 1995, with 89 wickets at 16.07, before taking his hundredth Test wicket, Graeme Hick's, against England at Johannesburg later in the year. Decisive efforts came regularly during a Test career that included twenty five-wicket hauls and ten wickets in a game on three occasions.

When he dominated it was usually in a winning cause, including his five for 74 at Lord's in 1994; eight for 71 at Harare in 1995-96; five for 46 against England at Cape Town in the same season; five for 40 and four for fourteen against India at Durban in 1996-97; and five for 36 against Australia at Centurion the following year.

Perhaps his finest series was in England in 1998 when he took 33 wickets at nineteen runs each in the series and had second innings figures of six for 88 from 40 overs at Old Trafford. England somehow survived to draw the game, and won the next at Trent Bridge when Donald unleashed a furious barrage of thrilling fast bowling on Mike Atherton after being denied two wickets by umpiring errors. At such times he was simply magnificent, win or lose.

82. ANDREW FLINTOFF

Andrew Flintoff, b. 6 December 1977, Preston

First-class: 8,739 runs (34.13), 331 wickets (31.64) and 180 catches
Tests (75): 3,645 runs (31.69), 218 wickets (32.07) and 51 catches
One-day internationals (138): 3,391 runs (32.60), 163 wickets (24.69)
and 43 catches

From 2004 to 2006 Andrew Flintoff took 111 wickets at 24.93, and scored 1,607 runs at 40.17 in 27 Tests. The all-round inspiration for England's captivating success in the 2005 Ashes series, he was in every sense a giant during this time and his efforts made him a very rich man. Either side of these golden years his prodigious natural talent was stifled first by his dilettante attitude in an era of stern profession-alism, then by persistent injuries and the stress of captaining a losing team in Australia.

A big, genial Lancashire lad from Preston with a sunny tempera-ment and abundant courage, he is the spiritual son of the Anglo-Australian Sammy Woods in the carefree days of the Edwardian era, or more recently of another Australian all-rounder, Keith Miller. Like Miller, he would have been a great companion in wartime, whether in action or in the bar. A schoolboy prodigy, Flintoff found it hard to accept the discipline demanded by the modern game, but he buckled down to shed weight from his mighty frame to do for England in 2005 what Ian Botham had in 1981.

He bowled long, inspirational spells at speeds touching 90 mph to take 24 wickets in the five Tests, scored 402 runs, including a brilliant century at Trent Bridge, and swallowed vital catches in the slips with consummate ease. Always a generous soul, the consolation that he offered to a shattered Brett Lee after England's desperate two-run victory at Edgbaston became the defining image for both this series and the game's true spirit.

In 2005-06, he played four important innings of 50 or more in a drawn Test series in India and proved an inspirational and tactically astute captain in the absence of the injured Michael Vaughan. Being asked to lead the side in Australia the following winter with a suspect ankle was, however, a bridge too far. Australia won 5-0, and although Flintoff bowled bravely through his pain, his batting was a huge disappointment. The side rallied to win the one-day series at the end of a traumatic tour, but the captain was disciplined for arriving at a practice unfit, having drunk into the early hours of the morning.

A long and often lonely fight to get back to full fitness ended with a successful return to the England side in 2008, following a fourth ankle operation that had become necessary because of a failed come-back the previous year. As it always had, his extra class made all the

difference to the one-day team that beat South Africa after losing the Test series, but his had already been a career spoiled by injuries.

In 2000, he had missed part of the West Indies series because of a stress fracture in his back. There were more back problems in 2001, followed by a hernia operation and an injury to his right shoulder in 2003. Each time, he battled back with fortitude and no signs of self-pity, but in the West Indies in 2009 the misery returned. He broke down with hip pain during the third Test at the Antigua Recreation Ground. As usual, it did not prevent his bowling as fast as he could in what turned out to be a vain attempt to bowl England to victory.

Signed for the Indian Premier League only a few weeks earlier for a salary of $1.55 million US, his future was again in jeopardy. If his playing career was to last much longer, the lesser strains of one-day cricket were likely to take precedence over the first-class game that had brought him greater satisfaction.

81. BILL PONSFORD

William Harold Ponsford, b. 19 October 1900, Melbourne; d. 6 April 1991, Kyneton, Victoria

First-class: 13,819 runs (65.18) and 71 catches
Tests (29): 2,122 runs (48.22) and 21 catches

Bill Ponsford, 'Ponny' to Victorians, was a rugged run machine, equalled only by Walter Hammond and, naturally, Don Bradman, during the general run spree in world cricket between the wars. He remains the only batsman to have played two first-class innings in excess of 400 runs; against Tasmania, 429 in 1922-23, and against Queensland, 437 in 1927-28. Both innings were played at the Melbourne Cricket Ground (MCG), where a huge depiction of him

in action now stands sentinel near one of the entrances to the vast arena that was once his playground.

The flatter the pitch the better he was, and the reverse was true too; but it is a further indication of his prowess that he was associated in the public mind with three different partners: Bill Woodfull, with whom he shared twenty partnerships of 100 or more; Bradman, with whom he put on 338 at Headingley and a record 451 at the Oval in his last two Tests in 1934; and Edgar Mayne, who shared an opening partnership of 456 against Queensland at Melbourne in 1923-24.

His Test career started in the middle order in 1924-25 with centuries in his first two games, at Sydney and Melbourne. He made five more in his 29 Tests, including 183 in the second Test against the West Indies at Sydney in 1930-31 and 266 in his last match at the Oval.

Nine of his thirteen scores in excess of 200 were for Victoria. He finished his career with a Shield average of 83.27 and an aggregate of 5,413 runs from 43 games. Had it not been for Bradman, such figures might have been described as 'Ponsfordesque'.

Sturdy and broad in the beam, Ponsford's movements appeared heavy, but they were deceptive. Footwork was the key to his batting, as it is with all great players. He milked the spinners into gaps in the field, often from well out of his crease. Even in defence against quick bowling, his bat and pad were so close that he was able to play the ball late for singles and twos. Only against the extreme pace of Harold Larwood in 1928-29 and 1932-33 was his batting a disappointment. In three tours of England he made over 4,000 runs, despite being picked for only the last two Tests in 1926 and scoring only 37 from his three innings.

The power of his concentration and his hunger for runs were extraordinary. When he played the ball onto his stumps after making 352 for Victoria against New South Wales at the MCG in 1926, he looked round in disgust and muttered to the wicket-keeper: 'How unlucky can you get?'

He made up for such outrageous fortune the following season. In December 1927 alone he scored 1,146 runs in five Sheffield Shield innings, at an average of 229.

80. C.B. FRY

Charles Burgess Fry, b. 25 April 1872, West Croydon; d. 7 September 1956, London

First-class: 30,886 runs (50.22), 166 wickets (29.34) and 240 catches
Tests (26): 1,233 runs (32.18) and seventeen catches

H.S. Altham said of C.B. Fry that 'alike in form and feature, he could have stepped out of the frieze of the Parthenon'. He was not only one of the most prolific of all batsmen, but also a polymath. He was a brilliant, domineering conversationalist and as a classical scholar he was placed ahead of the future Lord Chancellor, F.E. Smith, at Wadham College, Oxford. For 21 years he was the joint holder of the world long-jump record after a leap of 23 feet, 6.5 inches in 1893, and he was an England footballer who won an FA Cup medal for Southampton in 1902, two days before scoring 82 for London County against Surrey at the Oval. But for an injury just before the University match, he would have added a rugby Blue to those that he won for athletics, cricket and soccer.

If his subsequent life, almost inevitably, was not quite so gilded, he ran a naval training ship, *TS Mercury*, on the Hamble River, wrote several excellent books on cricket, edited a magazine, served with the League of Nations and turned down an invitation to rule Albania in lieu of King Zog.

Fry played for four years in the Repton and Oxford cricket teams, captaining both. Having made a hundred in the 1894 match against Cambridge, he played one match for Surrey, the county of his birth, then for Sussex from 1891 until his move to the *Mercury* in 1909 prompted him to play his last season for Hampshire. Now 49, he was asked by the England selectors to play against the all-conquering Australians but declined.

In six seasons he had topped the national batting averages, hitting

thirteen hundreds, including a then record of six in succession, in 1901. That year he scored 3,147 runs. His 232 not out at Lord's in 1903 was the highest score ever made for the Gentlemen in the longstanding fixture against the Players. Of his 94 first-class hundreds, sixteen were doubles. Concentration was never a problem.

Although he was not always a success in Tests he made two memorable hundreds at the Oval, against Australia in 1905 and two seasons later against the South African googly bowlers who had been bamboozling his colleagues. He led England to success in the triangular series against Australia and South Africa in 1912.

79. MAHELA JAYAWARDENE

Denegamage Proboth Mahela de Silva Jayawardene, b. 27 May 1977, Colombo

First-class: 13,960 runs (52.28), 51 wickets (30.90) and 232 catches
Tests (102): 8,251 runs (53.23), five wickets (54.60) and 142 catches
One-day internationals (299): 8,042 runs (32.03), seven wickets (79.71)
and 159 catches

Although he may not have quite the innate genius of Aravinda De Silva, Sri Lanka's first great batsman of their international era, nor the wiliness of Arjuna Ranatunga, the captain who convinced his players that they need fear no one, Mahela Jayawardena is likely to surpass the achievements of both. He is a batsman of polished technical perfection with the cool, calculating temperament and quiet dignity of a great leader.

As with all the finest batsmen the ball seems always to come to him, rather than he to go looking for it. Only when occasionally tempted to chase something wide does he look vulnerable, but his

eyes and feet are generally in perfect harmony. He is brave, too, and shrewd, both in planning an innings and in dealing with the politicians who meddle in Sri Lankan cricket. By 2009 he was ready to hand those responsibilities to someone else.

In his first Test in 1997-98 at the Premadasa Stadium in Colombo he went into bat when Sri Lanka were 790 for four against India. He made 66. Soon afterwards, against New Zealand, he played a mature and accomplished innings of 167 at Galle on a far less friendly pitch for batsmen. A marathon 242 against India followed in his seventh Test, and apart from a dip in his form and confidence in 2002-03 he has been a pillar of the side ever since.

His leadership qualities were first recognised in England in 2006, when he deputised for Marvan Atapattu and batted with infinite patience for scores of 61 and 119 to help to save a Lord's Test that had seemed irretrievable. Later that year, on his favourite playground, the Sinhalese Sports Club in Colombo, he scored 374 against South Africa and shared in a world record partnership of 624 with Kumar Sangakkara.

Almost as prolific in one-day cricket, he led his side to the final of the 2007 World Cup, scoring 115 off 109 balls in the semi-final against New Zealand, all by means of artistry rather than force.

A superb close catcher, whether to fast bowlers or slow, he had taken 68 catches off Muttiah Muralitharan alone by the end of 2008, a record for a fielder off the same bowler.

78. COLIN COWDREY

Michael Colin Cowdrey, b. 24 December 1932, Ootacamund, India; d. 4 December 2000, Angmering, Sussex

First-class: 42,719 runs (42.89), 65 wickets (51.21) and 638 catches
Tests (114): 7,624 runs (44.06) and 120 catches

Few batsmen in the game's history have had a more felicitous touch than Colin Cowdrey, a gentle master of the batting art who, as Hubert Doggart said, really did 'time the ball like an angel'. His great contribution to the game that dominated his life was celebrated by a packed congregation at his memorial service in Westminster Abbey. By the time of his death in 2000 this son of an Indian-based tea-broker had become Lord Cowdrey of Tonbridge. No one had given more of himself or his time to the cause of the game that he revered.

Born in the hills above Bangalore he was rapidly introduced to golf and cricket by Ernest, the games-playing father who had foretold his son's destiny by giving him the initials MCC. Colin's rich talent was rapidly fulfilled when he went to school in England. He played for Tonbridge against Clifton at Lord's as a podgy little thirteen-year-old leg-spinner, not only taking eight for 117 but scoring 75 and 44.

This was the stuff of schoolboy yarns and he became the first man to play 100 Tests, the sixteenth to score 100 first-class hundreds – he made 107 in all, the last in a glorious run chase for Kent to beat the 1975 Australians – and captain of England 27 times. Reckoned to be an indecisive leader, he was also a sympathetic one, and he enjoyed a notable triumph in the West Indies in 1967-68 before the great disappointment of suffering a snapped Achilles tendon early the following season prevented him from leading England in an Ashes series. In all he toured Australia six times, but never as captain.

The last of his visits, three years after what had been assumed to be his last Test, was as a willing replacement for John Edrich and Dennis Amiss, both of whom had broken their hands in the first Test batting against the ferocious Lillee and Thomson in 1974-75. Fresh from an English winter, the venerable Cowdrey was plunged into the deep four days after his arrival on the fastest pitch in the world, the WACA at Perth. 'How do you do,' he said on reaching the crease to face Thomson. 'I don't think we've met. My name's Cowdrey.' 'In the middle of a bloody Test match. I couldn't bloody believe it,' recalled 'Thommo'. More than two hours later Cowdrey, 41 years old in his 110th Test, was bowled for 22 by Thomson, 24 years old in his third Test.

The young Cowdrey's progress into the England team had been swift, despite a relatively modest three years in the Oxford side that had included a century in the 1953 match against Cambridge. For

Kent he had made 90 against Hampshire and 71 against the South Africans as an eighteen-year-old, becoming the youngest capped player of the county that he was to lead for fifteen seasons. Winning the Championship with a surge in the second half of the season in 1970 was the highlight.

His natural charm and kindness masked great determination when the chips were down. Despite hearing of his father's death on the ship to Australia in 1954, he played one of the great Test innings in inimical circumstances at Melbourne, 102 out of 191. He scored 21 more Test centuries, including the influential 154 against the West Indies in 1957 when he shared a stand of 411 with Peter May that laid the bogey of Sonny Ramadhin's mysterious spin. His plan in that innings, padding away balls outside the off stump, led to a change in the LBW law to penalise batsmen not attempting a shot with the bat.

He was prone to periods of introspection about his technique, but they were not necessary. Brought up to stroke the ball through the off side, he also became the surest of hookers against quick bowling and had a wonderfully deft touch against spinners, including a paddle shot hit to fine leg with a straight bat. Despite having small hands he was a wonderfully reliable catcher at first slip.

Constantly writing messages of encouragement to young cricketers in neat handwriting on postcards, he served on numerous committees, was president of MCC in 1986-87 and, as chairman of the ICC from 1989 to 1993, was chiefly responsible for making the old boys' alliance of England and Australia a genuinely international body representing the wider world and reflecting the commercial reality of modern professional sport. As with his cricket, there was an iron fist within the velvet glove.

77. MAURICE TATE

Maurice William Tate, b. 29 April 1895, Brighton, Sussex; d. 18 May 1956, Wadhurst, Sussex

First-class: 21,717 runs (25.02) 2,784 wickets (18.16) and 284 catches
Tests (39): 1,198 runs (25.48) 155 wickets (26.16) and eleven catches

I remember the day that Maurice Tate died in 1956 because the PE teacher at my school in Eastbourne came into my dormitory overwhelmed by the news, and in a hushed voice began to recall some of his deeds. 'Chub' Tate was a Sussex legend and one of the finest and cheeriest of all the cricketers of his day. He was a considerable batsman, good enough to open in county cricket and to pass 1,000 runs in twelve seasons, but it is as a fast-medium bowler without equal in his era that he chiefly excelled.

He took no fewer than 848 wickets between 1922 and 1925.

For a few years either side of the First World War he had been more of a batting all-rounder who bowled useful slow medium offbreaks, very similar to those of his one-Test father Fred. Quite suddenly this gave way to a permanent role as a waspish new-ball bowler who swerved and bounced it off the seam more venomously than many a bowler who ran in further or was faster through the air.

Having bowled a well-set Phil Mead with a vicious cutter off his short run at Eastbourne in 1922, Tate proved in the nets that it had been no fluke and took the advice of his captain, Arthur Gilligan, to bowl more quickly all the time. The results were startling. Against Middlesex he took the first five wickets to reduce them to 26 for five, and in the last two months of the season he took 50 wickets. The following year he was a sensation, a 28-year-old county stalwart suddenly transformed into a potential world-beater, who surprised everyone by his kicking pace off the pitch. He took his 100th wicket on 16 June and finished the season with 219 wickets at under fourteen.

Gilligan and Tate were the talk of sporting England in 1924. They bowled out Surrey for 53 in just over an hour. Soon after, in Tate's first Test at Edgbaston, they combined to wreck South Africa in 45 minutes for 30, sharing nineteen of the twenty wickets in the two innings. The Sussex pair were fully expected to counter Gregory and McDonald on the next tour of Australia until Gilligan was hit over the heart when batting in the Gentlemen vs. Players match, and was badly enough hurt never to find the same pace again.

He still led the side to Australia, where Tate dumbfounded those who thought that his transformation had been exaggerated. In the first Test at Sydney he bowled 88 eight-ball overs, the equivalent of 117.2 today, for a return of eleven for 228. A pulped big toe was the cost, but he bowled through the pain in the second game at Melbourne, soldiering on through another 78.3 eight-ball overs for nine more wickets. In both cases his efforts were in vain, but Australia were beaten in the fourth Test with Tate taking five wickets in the second innings. He finished the series with 38 wickets, a record that stood for almost 30 years.

Alec Bedser was in the Tate mould and so, to some extent, was the Lancashire and England bowler Ken Higgs. All were strong men with powerful thighs. Tate, like Bedser after him, had powerful shoulders, as well as big feet that were famously caricatured by Tom Webster. His walk was rolling but, once he turned clockwise on his mark, everything was an exercise in smooth momentum. Ian Peebles left a vivid description of his action:

He ran in briskly, a distance of about eight yards. At the crease he started his swing leaning well back on his right leg with his left arm fully extended. The bend of his back and the roll of his shoulders brought his right arm catapulting over with a smooth elasticity which gave an impression of immense momentum. In Australia his slips stood considerably deeper than they did to the accredited fast bowlers.

Universally popular, he was given to spoonerisms. He once described his appalled reaction after a ball had just missed the off stump for the third time in succession: 'I just stood there nude.'

76. ANDY FLOWER

Andrew Flower, b. 28 April 1968, Cape Town, South Africa

First-class: 16,379 runs (54.75), 361 catches and 36 stumpings
Tests (63): 4,794 runs (51.94), 151 catches and nine stumpings
One-day internationals (213): 6,786 runs (35.34), 141 catches and 32
stumpings

The outstanding figure in Zimbabwe's brief hour in the cricketing sun, Andy Flower was an exemplary professional who added to the highest of reputations as a player by standing up to the tyranny of Robert Mugabe's regime with a public stand during the 2003 World Cup.

He and his black team-mate, the multi-talented fast bowler Henry Olonga, took the field for Zimbabwe in the televised match against Namibia in Harare wearing black armbands, having issued a statement 'mourning the death of democracy in our beloved Zimbabwe'. Defying both the country's one-party government and the ICC, they wore black wristbands for the next game. For Olonga it meant the end of a short career. For Flower the sacrifice was smaller, perhaps, but it meant leaving his home country at the age of 34 and setting up a new life as a professional for Essex and also, briefly, South Australia.

A neat, slim left-handed batsman of below medium height, he possessed great skill, tenacity, self-discipline and intelligence. He paced his innings with much the same care and shrewdness whether he was opening or batting down the order. He was also a fine wicket-keeper, although he handed on the gloves for a time when he felt that his form was being affected by captaincy.

Flower was coached at Vainona High School, Harare, and by his father, Bill. His younger brother Grant was also a highly effective international and county cricketer. Andy determined to become a professional when he toured England with a club side at the age of sixteen. Further experience in league cricket was followed by success in the ICC trophy in Holland. Zimbabwe's third successive win in this tournament led to an official place at the top table at just the right time for him. He batted through the innings for 115 not out in their first official one-day international but it was in a losing cause, an experience that was to become familiar.

Succeeding the other main trailblazer, David Houghton, Flower was captain when Zimbabwe won a Test for the first time, against Pakistan in Harare in February 1995. He scored 156 in his only innings, and his brother Grant a double century. He played in each of his country's first 52 Tests and 172 internationals, a sequence that ended only when he broke a thumb.

He lost the captaincy after the tour of England in 2000 to Zimbabwe's other outstanding cricketer, Heath Streak, but responded typically with a run spree. In nine Tests, Flower made 1,066 runs at an average of 88, including the highest score by a wicket-keeper in a Test, 232 not out at Nagpur. On that tour he outdid the Indians at their own patient game, making at least 50 in his four Test innings and 183 not out in the first of them. Against South Africa in the first Test at Harare in September 2001, he kept throughout a ten-hour innings without conceding a bye, then scored 142 and 199 not out in virtually isolated defiance as South Africa were defeated by an innings. It was the stuff of heroism.

His experience and human qualities were invaluable to Essex in the last phase of his playing career before he took on the job of England's chief batting coach in 2007 and acting head coach in the West Indies in 2009.

75. E.R. DEXTER

Edward Ralph Dexter, b. 15 May 1935, Milan

First-class: 21,150 runs (40.75), 419 wickets (29.93) and 234 catches
Tests (62): 4,502 runs (47.89), 66 wickets (34.93) and 29 catches

Ted Dexter was something of an enigma, but in the right mood he was a batsman playing on a plane so exalted, and with an air of such

cool command, that he roused visions of Shelley's appropriately enigmatic visionary poem: 'My name is Ozymandias, King of Kings: look on my works, ye mighty, and despair.'

Also a champion amateur golfer, twice winner of the President's Putter at Rye, he was one of the finest all-round games-players of any generation. When he put his mind to applying the full imperious quality of his batting, he could dominate any attack with clean, full-bladed classical driving off either foot.

Born in Italy of English parents, he was handsome and effortlessly athletic but never really enjoyed the close attention that his brilliance attracted. The popular newspapers dubbed him 'Lord Ted' or 'Lord Edward' and many thought him arrogant: in fact he was shy and unusually vague. Like Colin Cowdrey, his near-contemporary and another supremely gifted player, he was a restless theoriser about cricket but would probably have been even more successful if he had batted by instinct.

A more settled position in the batting order would also have helped. He started his England career (like many apprentices) at number six, then batted at five, three and five again in the next three games. As captain in Australia in 1962-63, he started the series at three with scores of 70, 99, 93 and 52 (run out) but the cares of leadership were such that he changed places, allowing Ken Barrington to take over with even greater success at first wicket down in the last two games. Despite that, he scored seven of his nine Test hundreds from that position, five of them in excess of 170.

Proving the substance in his batting that Australians had doubted when he was rushed out as an undergraduate to supplement the England batting reserves in 1958-59, he played two long defensive innings to deny Australia expected victories: 180 at Edgbaston in 1961 and 174 in eight hours at Old Trafford in 1964. His highest score was 205 against Pakistan in Karachi on the long tour of the subcontinent in 1961-62, when he captained with distinction.

Yet he is best remembered for two innings that fell short of winning a game for England. These were the dazzling 76 made against Australia at Old Trafford in 1961, when Dexter seemed to have assured England of victory in the fourth innings only for Richie Benaud to steal the game and the Ashes; and, two years later, the thunderous 70 against Wes Hall and Charlie Griffith at Lord's that still glows in the memory of every witness.

Dexter captained Cambridge in 1958, and Sussex from 1960 to 1965, leading them to inventive successes in the first two Gillette Cup finals at Lord's. Also a superb fielder and an explosive fast-medium bowler off a short run, he was a genuine box-office draw and his life beyond the cricket field was richer than most, often to the delight of the newspapers. He rode motorbikes, flew private planes and owned racehorses and greyhounds. Married to a model, he himself modelled clothes, ran a PR company, wrote and broadcast on cricket, stood unsuccessfully as a Conservative candidate in Cardiff against the future prime minister James Callaghan, and was the professional chairman of the England committee from 1989 to 1993.

74. RAHUL DRAVID

Rahul Sharad Dravid, b. 11 January 1973, Indore, Madhya Pradesh

First-class: 20,303 runs (55.17), five wickets (54.60), 312 catches and one stumping
Tests (131): 10,509 runs (52.28), one wicket (39.00) and 180 catches
One-day internationals (333): 10,585 runs (39.49), 193 catches and fourteen stumpings

The contemporary of Sachin Tendulkar, Sourav Ganguly, V.V.S. Laxman and Virender Sehwag, Rahul Dravid was a model of consistency in an era when India always had a strong batting side and was gradually becoming the most powerful cricketing nation. Like his great contemporaries, he became rich, supported by a huge, widely disseminated and increasingly affluent population whose passion for the game has been equalled only, perhaps, in Barbados.

People like to knock top dogs but, like Tendulkar and his successor as captain, Anil Kumble, Dravid has been a perfect ambassador for his country and for cricket in general. Intelligent and disciplined, he was seldom an exciting batsman to watch in his early days but his right-handed technique, with the ball played late and the weight of his body always on top of the ball, became the most watertight of any batsman in the world in the early years of the twenty-first century. As Billy Woodfull was called the 'Unbowlable', Dravid was the 'Wall'.

He has never done a graceless thing on a cricket field, and technically and morally has been such an example to other players that it was surprising that he should have captained India for a relatively short period, between 2005 and 2008. As one of those players who worry and work at their game, however, he was happier in a supporting role. Such is his conscientious approach to life that he would have made a success of any profession. He completed a degree in commerce at Bangalore, despite having played for Karnataka at the age of eighteen, making a century in his second game.

Having just missed a century, with 95, in his first Test for India at Lord's in 1996, when Ganguly, also in his first appearance, shared a long stand, he made his first forward surge as a one-day player, enjoying partnerships in excess of 300 with both Ganguly and Tendulkar in 1999.

Dravid's form and character were integral to India's gradual improvement in confidence and consistency. He shared with Laxman the great and scintillating partnership of 376 for the fifth wicket at Calcutta (now Kolkata) that turned the best short series of modern times, against Australia early in 2001. He made a chanceless 180 in the second innings after India had followed on, before being run out.

By now established at number three, he played saving innings in Tests at Port Elizabeth, Georgetown and Trent Bridge and centuries that led to victories at Leeds, Adelaide, Kandy and Rawalpindi. A nation that had hitherto let itself down too often overseas was doing itself justice, largely through Ganguly's captaincy and Dravid's utter reliability. At his peak he scored four double centuries in fifteen Tests and between 2004 and 2008 he was, by a run or two, superior even to Tendulkar.

A superbly reliable first slip, he also kept wicket in 73 one-day internationals, albeit with no pretensions to great expertise.

73. MARTIN DONNELLY

Martin Paterson Donnelly, b. 17 October 1917, Ngaruawahia, New Zealand; d. 22 October 1999, Sydney

First-class: 9,250 runs (47.43), 43 wickets (39.13) and 76 catches
Tests (7): 582 runs (52.90), and seven catches

New Zealanders may argue the respective merits of Martin Donnelly and Bert Sutcliffe, the country's two greatest left-handed batsmen, and compare them with the much admired Test captain of a more recent era, Stephen Fleming. Those who were contemporaries of Martin Donnelly were in no doubt, however. He is bracketed with Sutcliffe, Martin Crowe and John Reid as the best of all New Zealand's batsmen and there is evidence that he was the most brilliant.

He was a superb all-round sportsman who played rugby for England against Ireland and produced several of the most memorable innings seen in big cricket just after the Second World War. C.B. Fry assessed him as at least the equal of any of the left-handers of his own long career, mentioning only Frank Woolley and Clem Hill in the same class. He was stocky, strong and quick on his feet, one of the great cover points but a brilliant fielder anywhere, and he had all the shots.

He went to England as a twenty-year-old in 1937 and scored 1,414 runs at 37. After war service as a tank commander in Egypt and Italy, he scored a glorious 133 for the Dominions against England at Lord's in 1945 and then became the great attraction in the Parks at Oxford. Geoffrey Bolton, the historian of Oxford cricket, wrote:

Bare figures can give no idea of the electric atmosphere in the Parks when that short, sturdy figure went out to bat. A lucky spectator might have half an hour to spare between lectures ... In that half hour he might well see Donnelly hit nine boundaries, each from a different stroke ... If Oxford were fielding the spectator's eyes would turn to cover point.

He scored another hundred at Lord's in the 1946 University match, in a legendary innings of 142 out of 261. As captain of Oxford in 1947 he scored a brilliant 162 not out in only three hours for the Gentlemen against the Players, so there was a certain inevitability when, as the batting star of the successful 1949 New Zealand touring team, he scored 208 in the Lord's Test. He averaged 77 in the series and scored 2,287 runs on the tour. Only A.P.F. Chapman also managed the same 'treble' of hundreds at Lord's: in a Test, Gents vs. Players and the University match.

While playing for Warwickshire against Middlesex in 1948, he was bowled by Jack Young when a ball spun off his boot, over his head and onto the back of the stumps. Such ill fortune was not, however, the reason for his early retirement. He had always played only as an amateur, and his job for the international company Courtaulds took him to Australia where, modest to a fault, he spoke about his lustrous sporting career only to those who asked. He played very little cricket after that, but he had left an indelible mark.

72. CLIVE LLOYD

Clive Hubert Lloyd, b. 31 August 1944, Georgetown, British Guiana

First-class: 31,232 runs (49.26), 114 wickets (36.00) and 377 catches
Tests (110): 7,515 runs (46.67), ten wickets (62.20) and 90 catches
One-day internationals (87): 1,977 runs (39.53), eight wickets (26.25)
and 39 catches

Like many other West Indies cricketers Clive Lloyd felt equally at home in Lancashire, where eventually he settled after a glittering county career that earned him the lasting affection of Mancunians especially. His imperishable claim to fame rests, however, on his

leadership of the most successful of all the West Indies sides. Under his benign-looking countenance and relaxed, even languid, demeanour lurked a very determined cricketer whose tactics on the field bore comparison with Douglas Jardine's for their single-minded pursuit of victory through fast bowling.

Lloyd himself gave immense pleasure as an attacking batsman and, in his youth, as a sensationally good cover fielder, with long arms, long ground-consuming strides and a deadly throw. He also bowled effectively at medium pace until his knees began to suffer from endless cricket. Very tall, with a shambling gait and a distracted air, and always batting in thick-rimmed glasses, he was an accomplished and thrilling left-handed batsman who drove, cut and hooked the ball with a heavy bat as hard as any man has. He and a number of other aspiring advanced-level coaches were once asked how to play a short, fast, rising ball on the off stump. Lloyd blinked at the responses of the other coaches, which ranged from a mimed ducking under the ball to a hasty backward defensive stroke, before rising onto the toes of his back foot to demonstrate a thunderous forcing shot past mid-off.

Attack was certainly his watchword and the drive his special glory, with a three-pound bat. His long career started for British Guiana in 1963-64, for Lancashire in 1968 and for the West Indies in India in 1966-67 when he scored 82 and 78 not out, a masterly innings on a turning pitch, in his first Test in Bombay. At home against England in 1967-68 he scored hundreds at Port of Spain and Bridgetown, his fielding prompting Alan Ross to describe him as 'a great, gangling begoggled supercat'. By 1975, when he made the most memorable of several wonderful centuries scored in a World Cup final, he bestrode Lord's like the colossus he was to play the innings that laid the basis of a close victory against Ian Chappell's no less formidable Australians. It was a glorious display of bold, powerful batting, played when international one-day cricket still had a freshness that appealed to all.

By the time that Lloyd led his team to a second triumph on the same ground against England in the second final, four years later, the cricket world had been irrevocably changed by Kerry Packer's World Series Cricket. There was more money at stake, and Lloyd and his team had lost their gay abandon.

The hardness in his cricket came partly from the experience of losing often in his early years as a Test player – his 132 in the Oval Test of 1973 helped to end a run of twenty Tests without a win – and partly from the attitude of Ian Chappell's Australian side, especially in the momentous series of 1975-76 when Dennis Lillee and Jeff Thomson got the better of a talented batting side, despite Lloyd's hundreds at Perth and Melbourne. There was an extra ruthlessness about the cricket that was played for two Australian seasons for the benefit of Packer's Channel Nine television station, by players earning far more than before; and the West Indies dominated world cricket, largely through the prowess of their fast bowlers, for the next twenty years.

With few exceptions, under Lloyd they went into each match with four fast bowlers, and by bowling relatively few overs they made themselves hard to beat. Lloyd always maintained that he picked his best bowlers whatever their speed. He led the West Indies in a record 74 Tests, winning 36 of them. Only two of his eighteen series in charge were lost. In 1985, this father figure handed the crown to Viv Richards.

71. JACK GREGORY

Jack Morrison Gregory, b. 14 August 1895, Sydney; died 7 August 1973, Bega, New South Wales

First-class: 5,661 runs (36.52), 504 wickets (20.99) and 195 catches
Tests (24): 1,146 runs (34.96), 85 wickets (31.15) and 37 catches

Jack Gregory was a spectacular, lusty, whole-hearted cricketer, the more explosive part of the most hostile pair of opening bowlers hitherto seen in Test cricket. With Ted McDonald he overwhelmed England immediately after the First World War, much as Ray Lindwall and Keith Miller were to do after the second.

In the words of R.C. Robertson-Glasgow, Gregory was 'tall, strong

and raw-boned, like one of his native kangaroos'. According to Ian Peebles he was 'towering, tanned and powerfully lithe'. Neville Cardus celebrated him as 'young manhood in excelsis'.

Gregory's very physical presence was too much for some batsmen. He bounded in off a twenty-yard run, and hurled the ball down after a high leap that covered the last three yards before delivery. As a left-handed batsman he hit hard, with low, skimming drives, using his long reach and sometimes playing without batting gloves. As a slip fielder he was brilliant, both to quick bowlers and to Arthur Mailey's leg breaks.

Part of a famous cricketing family, he made his name with the Australian forces side in England in 1919, for whom he scored almost 1,000 runs and took 131 wickets at 18.19. The AIF team went home via South Africa, where the 23-year-old giant added another 47 wickets at thirteen runs each. In his first official Test series in 1920-21 he took 23 wickets, scored 442 runs with a century at Sydney and caught fifteen catches in Australia's 5-0 victory.

His partnership with the graceful, equally fast but more accurate McDonald began in the third Test, and between them they were the driving force that extended Australia's run to eight Tests in succession a few months later in England. Those with long memories recalled, during the 'Bodyline' series in 1932-33, that the sound of ball on bone had been a familiar one in England twelve years earlier. Ernest Tyldesley was hit on the jaw and Frank Woolley in the kidney by rising balls from Gregory, whose 116 wickets on the tour included that of the young Walter Hammond, bowled by a ball quicker than any he had hitherto faced.

Gregory scored 1,135 runs on the tour, the performance of a serious batsman, not merely the hitter to whose name still stands the fastest Test hundred in terms of minutes, only 70, against South Africa at Johannesburg on the Old Wanderers ground in 1921-22. In that same series he took fifteen wickets at eighteen runs each on the matting pitches.

A knee injury curtailed Gregory's tour of England in 1926 and he broke down again in the next home series. McDonald, meanwhile, had chosen to play professionally in Lancashire after only eight Tests for Australia, so their partnership was as short-lived as it was spectacular.

70. DAVID GOWER

David Ivon Gower, b. 1 April 1957, Tunbridge Wells, Kent

First-class: 26,339 runs (40.09), four wickets (56.75), 280 catches and one stumping
Tests (117): 8,231 runs (44.25), one wicket (20.00) and 74 catches

It is curious that the man who briefly held the record as England's highest ever run scorer in Test cricket should often be remembered as being somehow an insubstantial player. Something in David Gower's nature prevented his being one of those men who can churn out a professional performance day in, day out. People looked forward to seeing him bat because he timed the ball with the touch of a concert pianist, and stroked it with a willowy grace. But because he made the game look easy, right from his first appearance for Leicestershire and England as a curly-haired boy who fielded brilliantly in the covers, there was special disappointment when he got himself out through what looked like carelessness.

When the occasion was big enough, he generally adorned it with left-handed batting that not only pleased the eye with its peculiar liquescence but also did the necessary job. Not only did he have quick reflexes, a sound technique and strokes all round the wicket, but the languid, frail look about his batting was deceptive: there was more inner grit than he ever wore on his sleeve.

Good-natured and resolutely casual, he liked to present himself as something of a playboy, but his true character was conventional and quite serious. Escapades such as driving a hired car onto ice in Switzerland only for it to sink, and escaping dressing-room duties on tour in Australia to go for a joy-ride in a Tiger Moth (persuading the local pilot to fly low over the ground on which England were playing) fitted the image more than they did the man.

He was an accomplished and capable captain who was officially appointed to the England job in 1984, having stood in for Bob Willis

in Pakistan the previous winter and enjoyed the challenge sufficiently to score 152 at Faisalabad and 173 not out in Lahore. His leadership setbacks in series against the mighty West Indies in 1984 and away in 1985-86 were due simply to the fact that he lacked the necessary counter-artillery.

The heavy reverse at home to Australia in 1989 was more serious, but it was balanced on the final account by a singular triumph in the previous home Ashes series and another in India in 1984-85, when England lost the first Test but won the series. 1985 was his high noon, one that followed a run of low scores in the international game that had disturbed his self-esteem and confidence more than he wished to show. He recovered his form with a century at Lord's in a one-day international, then made 732 glorious runs in the Test series, including innings of 166 at Trent Bridge, a rollicking 215 at Edgbaston and 157 at the Oval. The sun shone and England won the Ashes.

From the moment that Gower scored 58 in his first innings against Pakistan in 1978, having pivoted to pull his first ball from the otherwise anonymous Liaqat Ali for four, his Test average never dropped below 40. He scored more runs than any other batsman against the formidable West Indian fast bowlers on their own grounds in the 1980s – 746 at 43 from nine Tests.

He settled down to a prosperous family life in Hampshire, for whom he played the last four years of his county career, and became a cool and loquacious anchorman for Sky television's international cricket coverage.

69. ALAN KNOTT

Alan Philip Eric Knott, b. 9 April 1946, Belvedere, Kent

First-class: 18,105 runs (29.63), two wickets (43.50), 1,211 catches and 133 stumpings
Tests (95): 4,389 runs (32.75), 250 catches and nineteen stumpings

A wonderfully nimble little wicket-keeper with an impish genius and a fetish for fitness, Alan Knott was the best of his time, even when measured against outstanding contemporaries who included his two main predecessors, John Murray and Jim Parks, his successor, Bob Taylor, and his Australian rival Rodney Marsh.

With a face like Mr Punch, darting brown eyes and a ready, wide grin, the popular 'Knottie' enlivened Kent and England teams throughout a long career that would have produced even better figures but for long breaks, first when he joined several of the world's best players in Kerry Packer's World Series Cricket in 1977, and then when he decided to join an officially disapproved tour of South Africa in 1982, which led to a three-year suspension from the international game.

By 1977 he had run up 89 Tests since taking seven catches in his first Test against Pakistan at Trent Bridge, surpassing all previous wicket-keeping records and excelling on six overseas tours. His batting was quirky but frequently brilliant, and he was invaluable to England at number seven in an order that was too often short of runs. Five of his seventeen first-class hundreds came in Tests, where he played with discretion or panache according to the situation. He would have been ideal for Twenty20 cricket, because he invented his own strokes by swift adjustments of the feet and body.

Some of his finest innings were played in adversity. He counterattacked outrageously when Bob Massie was swinging the ball so prodigiously at Lord's in 1972; hit the spinners over the top to contribute much towards England's sporadic successes on his two tours of India; and was England's second-highest scorer when Dennis Lillee and Jeff Thomson proved too good for most on lively pitches in 1974-75.

His centuries at Adelaide during that series, and his precious 135 at Trent Bridge in the 1977 series against Australia, were his most satisfying innings, but throughout the 1970s he was also a key member of a successful Kent team, scoring two not out centuries in the same match for them against Surrey at Maidstone in 1972.

According to Derek Underwood, especially on drying pitches when the ball was turning and bouncing alarmingly, he was the perfect complement both for county and country, never appearing hurried. His alertness and agility were even more remarkable when he was standing back to the quick and medium-paced bowlers. Flinging himself to left or right, he reminded Kentish spectators of a certain age of the equally gymnastic but much more extroverted Godfrey Evans. On his day Evans was probably capable of even more but Knott was the more consistent.

68. WARWICK ARMSTRONG

Warwick Windridge Armstrong, b. 22 May 1879, Kyneton, Victoria; d. 13 July 1947, Sydney

First-class: 16,158 runs (46.83), 832 wickets (19.71) and 273 catches
Tests (50): 2,863 runs (38.69), 87 wickets (33.59) and 44 catches

Warwick Armstrong, graphically known as the 'Big Ship', had what Ian Peebles called 'a flair for success'. He never lost a game as Australia's captain, had immense confidence in his own ability and stood up unflinchingly for what he believed was right.

More than just an outstanding all-round player, he was a symbol of Australian independence. He took strong and effective stands on issues such as cricketers' pay – he was one of the six players who refused to tour England in 1912 because of the inadequate recompense being offered by the Australian Cricket Board – the crowded itineraries of touring teams; and his preference for timeless Tests to avoid boring draws, although these days his case might seem even more debatable. The famous story, embroidered a little by Arthur Mailey in his autobiography, that Armstrong picked up a newspaper blown in his direction in the outfield during the moribund fifth Test at the Oval in 1921 'to find out whom Australia were playing' is not strictly true – it was a leaflet featuring photographs of the players at which he glanced with interest for a while. But it is the sort of thing he might have said.

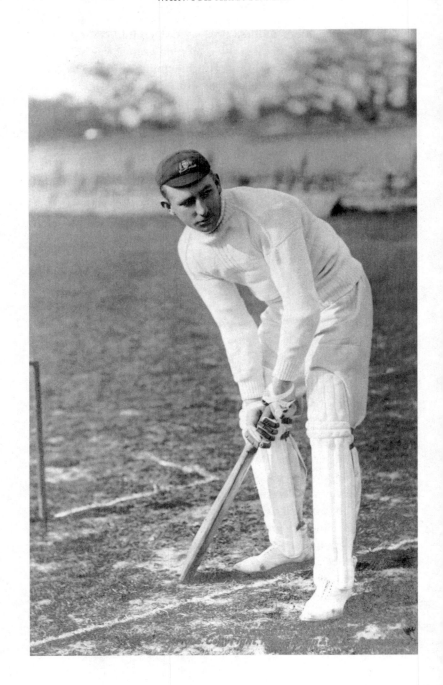

He did not set out to offend, but nor did he care if he did so.

His approach to the captaincy of Australia in the two one-sided series after the First World War, at home when England were beaten 5-0 and the following English summer when the margin was 3-0, was hard and uncompromising. He was a strong disciplinarian and pragmatic tactician for whom winning was the whole point, not necessarily the spirit in which the winning occurred. But – like many big men who assert their weight in every way – he was also generous, especially to children, and he mellowed in an old age that was wealthy as a consequence of his role in the success of the whisky company Distillers.

A tall, balanced and very accurate leg-spinner, slim in his youth but weighing twenty stone by the time he retired, he was a batsman who made full use of his reach but also square-cut mightily. He averaged 50 with the bat for Victoria in the Sheffield Shield, and 24 with the ball. He toured England in 1902, 1905, 1909 and 1921, making almost 6,000 runs and taking 443 wickets at 16.45, including analyses of five for 27 in the first Test at Edgbaston in 1909 and six for 35 in the second innings at Lord's. But his best tour was his second when he scored 303 not out against Somerset at Bath, made 2,002 runs in all and took 130 wickets at 17.60.

67. SANATH JAYASURIYA

Sanath Teran Jayasuriya, b. 30 June 1969, Matara, Sri Lanka

First-class: 14,742 runs (38.59), 205 wickets (32.77) and 162 catches
Tests (110): 6,973 runs (40.07), 98 wickets (34.34) and 78 catches
One-day internationals (427): 12,963 runs (32.65), 311 wickets (36.62) and 119 catches

One sign of greatness is genuine originality. Sanath Jayasuriya, whose presence in any match guaranteed entertainment while he was batting,

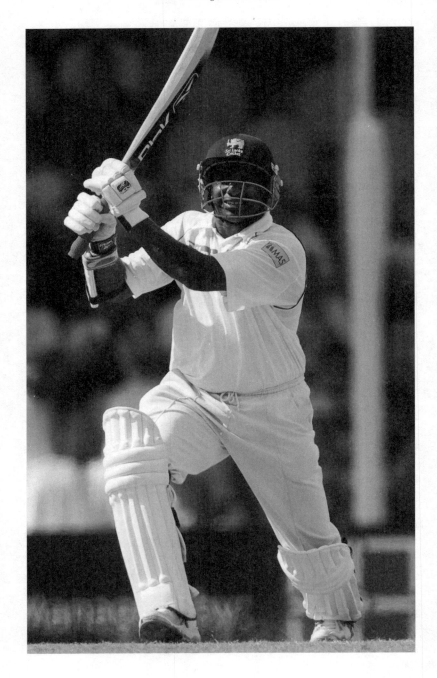

reinvented the approach to 50-over cricket, and by his talent and boldness made possible World Cup victory in 1996 for a nation whose love and aptitude for cricket had lain dormant too long.

The term 'pinch-hitting' as applied to cricket originates from Sri Lanka's strategy of attacking the new ball in the first fifteen overs of an innings during that tournament, while six fielders had to be kept within a 30-yard circle. It did not always come off for Jayasuriya and his opening partner Romesh Kaluwitharana, but on the bland pitches of the Indian subcontinent there was a good chance of recovery if it did not. Against India in Calcutta they took the wind out of the home team's sails by scoring 42 from the first three overs. Jayasuriya's best contribution was his 82 in the quarter-final against England, when he hit three sixes and thirteen fours before departing in the thirteenth over. A few weeks later he hit what was then the fastest one-day hundred, off 48 balls against Pakistan in Singapore, and the fastest 50, from seventeen.

A little butcher, left-handed and with strong wrists and forearms, Jayasuriya was one of the most destructive players of them all, especially when hitting square of the wicket on the off-side. His method was to wait in line with his leg stump before carving anything straight or outside the off stump, through or over the field between third-man and extra cover. Sixes rained from his bat in that region in most of his major innings. When bowlers tried to adjust by switching their line to his legs, he was quick to pull or scoop them over square-leg instead.

If Test cricket demanded more discretion he applied it, reluctantly and to a limited degree, but sufficiently to score fourteen Test hundreds. Born and raised in the fishing village of Matara on the south coast, an area badly hit by the tsunami in December 2004, he did not come from a traditional cricket background but his obvious talent flourished when Sri Lanka began playing first-class matches more widely in 1988-89, when Jayasuriya was nineteen. He established himself by scoring successive double centuries for Sri Lanka B against Pakistan B in Lahore and Karachi, and in 1995-56 made a maiden Test century at Adelaide.

In 1997 he scored 340 in response to a tall total by India at the Premadasa stadium in Colombo. In a match in which each partnership averaged 106, he and Roshan Mahanama added 576 for the second wicket. In his next Test Jayasuriya scored 199. The following year he played a glorious innings at the Oval, 213 from 278 balls with 33 fours and a six, buying time for Muttiah Muralitharan to win the match on a dry pitch after England had batted into the second afternoon.

The selectors prematurely retired him in 2006 but he returned in coloured clothes to score three successive hundreds – two against England, one against Holland – before announcing his own Test retirement the following year. Having done so, he hit a 26th one-day hundred on his 39th birthday in June 2008.

Throughout his career he was a useful slow left-arm bowler, varying his pace cleverly and spinning the ball sharply on turning pitches; and he was a sharp fielder close to the wicket.

66. JOHN SNOW

John Augustine Snow, b. 13 October 1941, Peopleton, Worcestershire

First-class: 4,832 runs (14.17), 1,174 wickets (22.72) and 125 catches
Tests (49): 772 runs (13.54), 202 wickets (26.66) and sixteen catches

John Snow has the visage of a Roman general, or perhaps of an ascetic monk, appropriate to the son of a vicar who christened him John Augustine. In his playing days there was a lean and hungry look about him, and his bowling had a mean streak in it that set him apart. Moody and competitive, he was a much better man to have on your own side than as an opponent.

Starting mainly as a batsman for Sussex and always an athletic out-fielder, he bowled some very quick balls and always hit the seam hard from a rhythmic, sturdy action that followed a relatively short,

relaxed, loping run. He varied his pace shrewdly, and quick bouncers were part of his stock in trade. He knew what he was doing, understood batsmen's frailties and feared no one.

He bowled especially well to left-handers, demonstrating that with several successes against Gary Sobers in his prime, getting him out when first he bowled at him in a Test in 1966, then dismissing him first ball at both the Oval, later in that series, and in the next Test between the two teams at Kingston.

He had been left out of England's strong team in Australia in 1965-66, having played his first two Tests the season before, then omitted again for the first two Tests of the 1966 home series against the West Indies. He responded by taking eleven for 47 against the touring team on a green, hard pitch at Hove, hustling them to defeat in two days.

He ought to have been an automatic selection for England after that, but experiments by selectors against lesser opposition occasionally meant that he was omitted, which annoyed him. Despite eventually becoming vice-chairman of Sussex, Snow was no great friend of committees. He was also dropped for knocking over Sunil Gavaskar as he tried to run him out in a Test at Lord's in 1971. When he returned to the team, he bowled Gavaskar for six in the first innings and had him LBW for nought in the second.

Between England's win against the West Indies at the Oval in 1966 and their defeat to India on the same ground four years later, England lost only once in 39 Tests. Snow took 113 wickets at 26 in the 28 matches he played in that period, spearheading the attack with flinty incisiveness.

His performances on hard wickets in the West Indies in 1967-68, when he took seven for 49 at Kingston and 27 wickets in his four Tests, and in Australia under Ray Illingworth in 1970-71, underlined his exceptional quality. He put the wind up his opponents in the first test at the Gabba and had sixteen wickets in the bag after two drawn games, before shooting Australia out for 116 in their second innings at Sydney, with figures of seven for 40. He fractured his bowling hand in the final Test but finished with 31 wickets at 22 in the series, the biggest single contribution to the regaining of the Ashes.

Writing in 1974 Dennis Lillee put Snow at the top of all the bowlers he had played with or against: 'Temperament, the ability to place the ball with precision, to make it cut off the wicket in England and lift sharply in Australia made him the champion he was.'

Having revealed his sensitive side by publishing two volumes of poetry, Snow set up his own successful travel business, specialising in sports tours.

65. STAN McCABE

Stanley Joseph McCabe, b. 16 July 1910, Grenfell, New South Wales

First-class: 11,951 runs (49.38), 159 wickets (33.72) and 139 catches
Tests (39): 2,748 runs (48.21), 36 wickets (42.86) and 41 catches

By the batting standards of his day Stan McCabe was not especially prolific, despite ending the 1931-32 season with a Sheffield Shield batting average of 438! Usually it took a crisis to bring out the champion in him, and that he was a great player is not in doubt. He proved it against the best fast bowling, and in three innings especially that transcended the prosaic and lived forever in the memories of witnesses.

Perfectly balanced, he was renowned not only as a beautiful driver of the ball but also as one of the boldest of all hookers. From his first Test in 1930 to his last in 1938 he was never left out of an Australia side, not least because of his ability to bowl fast-medium well enough sometimes to be given the new ball. The astonishing fast googly that bowled Walter Hammond in the deciding Test at the Oval in 1930 was arguably the most important ball of the series.

At Sydney in the opening Test of the 1932-33 series, when Australia found a fresh Harold Larwood too good for them, McCabe was the exception. Cutting and hooking with relish, he steered his side from 87 for four to 290 for five by the close of the first day, scoring 130 not

out. The next morning, as the tail crumbled, a series of thrilling strokes took him to 187 not out. He scored 60 of the team's last 70 runs.

On tour in England in 1934 he scored eight centuries and more than 2,000 first-class runs, upstaged only by Don Bradman, and in the Tests scored 483 runs at 60. There followed in 1935-36 in Johannesburg a sensational innings played with such ferocity in such poor light after a dust storm that South Africa's captain, Herbie Wade, appealed against the light on the ground that McCabe's assault was threatening the safety of the fielders.

Australia had been set 299 to win on a turning pitch, but on the final morning McCabe made 100 before lunch. Play was called off three hours early, with McCabe 189 not out in a total of 274 for two.

His third spectacular is the most famous, the innings at Trent Bridge in 1938 when Bradman begged his colleagues to come onto the balcony to watch because they would see nothing like it again. Nineteen not out at the start of the third day, and in the face of a huge England total, McCabe took his score to 232 in 235 minutes with 30 fours and a six. He was last out, having scored 72 of a last-wicket partnership of 77 with 'Chuck' Fleetwood-Smith.

The son of a barber and one of four cricket-playing boys, McCabe ran a successful sports shop in George Street, Sydney after the war. Asked why he had not written any memoirs he replied: 'I never hated anyone enough.' Convalescing after a long spell in hospital, he died accidentally from a fall over a cliff at Mosman.

64. LES AMES

Leslie Ethelbert George Ames, b. 3 December 1905, Elham, Kent; d. 22 February 1990, Canterbury

First-class: 37,248 runs (43.51), 703 catches and 418 stumpings
Tests (47): 2,434 runs (40.56), 74 catches and 23 stumpings

Dark-eyed and brown as a nut from his Romany blood and years in the sun, and with a personality as bubbly as champagne, Les Ames was a star in an age of cricket quite different from the present one. Yet he would have been a priceless asset in the era of one-day and, not least, Twenty20 cricket because he was both a top-class wicket-keeper and a dashing attacking batsman who played especially well against spinners.

The only wicket-keeper to have scored 100 first-class hundreds (102 in all), and one of only four genuine all-rounders among the 25 cricketers who have achieved this feat, he has two other records that are unlikely ever to be surpassed: in 1932 he stumped 64 of his 100 victims; and in his career 415.

His accomplice in 259 of those stumpings was the diminutive wizard of leg-breaks and googlies 'Tich' Freeman, who was to Kent in the years between the wars what Mushtaq Ahmed was to Sussex over a much shorter span in the 2000s. Thanks to Freeman, no English wicket-keeper has spent so much time up to the stumps as Ames. In 1928 he combined 122 dismissals with 1,919 runs; the following season 128 dismissals with 11,795 runs. His 100 victims in 1934 could be added to 2,482 runs. No wonder he always made cricket look such fun.

As a batsman his approach was always to attack if possible and, blessed with nimble footwork, he was never afraid to be stumped himself. Caught in the deep on one occasion off the renowned Gloucestershire off-spinner Tom Goddard, he said with a smile to one of the fielders: 'I'd rather be caught there than at short-leg.' Godfrey Evans, Kent and England's still more brilliant wicket-keeper after the war, called him 'Twinkletoes', adding: 'I'd never seen a major batsman play so far out of his crease.'

He played for Kent from 1926, as well as soccer for Gillingham. His cricket career flourished until the outbreak of the Second World War and then, mainly as a batsman, for five full seasons after it. He made 105 in the second innings of his third game for England, at Port of Spain in 1929-30, and added a second century – his highest, 149 – at Kingston. Once he had won the selection battle between himself and George Duckworth (the familiar argument of wicket-keeper/batsman versus pure 'keeper), he was the regular choice throughout the 1930s.

Ames remained in professional cricket until old age. He was a national selector from 1950 to 1956 – and therefore a party to the recalls of Cyril Washbrook, David Sheppard and Denis Compton in the last, Ashes-winning, year – and the secretary/manager of Kent during their successful years in the 1970s. He also managed three MCC tours and was president of Kent.

63. STEVE WAUGH

Stephen Rodger Waugh, b. 2 June 1965, Sydney

First-class: 24,052 runs (51.94), 249 wickets (32.75) and 273 catches
Tests (168): 10,927 runs (51.06), 92 wickets (37.44) and 112 catches
One-day-internationals (325): 7,569 runs (32.90), 195 wickets (34.67)
and 111 catches

Steve Waugh was so tough that it was easy to overlook his class. As a youngster for New South Wales, he struck a ball from a fast bowler with such clean ease into the upper reaches of a stand at extra cover that the watching Alan Davidson was convinced, there and then, that a great batsman had emerged. In later years he was eclipsed in terms of grace and poise by Mark Waugh, who briefly took his twin brother's place in Australia's batting line-up before they joined forces to great effect for many years. But Steve hardly cared how elegant his batting looked, so long as he did the job for his side.

His record for Australia is evidence enough of a high-class batsman of extraordinary durability, but his fame rests also upon inventive, confident captaincy that would never admit that any Australia side could be second-best until a game was finally lost. Under Waugh it seldom was: Australia won a then record of sixteen Test matches in succession between 1999 and 2001; and 41 of his 57 Tests in charge. They also won 67 of his 106 one-day internationals as captain.

He was blessed to have two match-winning bowlers, Glenn

McGrath and Shane Warne, plus a number of dominating batsmen, but he made it his business as captain to encourage fast scoring. He reasoned that if Australia scored substantial totals at four runs an over there would almost always be time to bowl the opposition out twice, even on good pitches. He also insisted that his teams should understand and respect the game's tradition and heritage.

While they reflected his own never-say-die approach to cricket, Australian teams under Waugh also benefited from his enlightenment as a man. As Tim May expressed it in his foreword to the 700-page autobiography that Waugh wrote without the usual recourse to a journalist's assistance, he was a leader 'able to educate and influence both young and old team members about the balance needed in life and the relevance of the plight of others. He is a person who inspires and invites mateship, respect, unselfishness and loyalty.'

Famously, Waugh never wore any other cap for Australia except the battered baggy green first awarded to him for a Test against India in 1986-87. Always a fast and committed fieldsman, he made the first of his many indelible marks on English opponents when his thoughtful medium-paced bowling earned him five for 69 in Perth. He changed his pace skilfully in the closing stages of the closely-fought World Cup final against England at Calcutta in 1987, a game that seemed to kick-start Australia's long period of success under Allan Border, Mark Taylor, Waugh and Ricky Ponting.

Waugh's part in the 1989 regaining of the Ashes in England was crucial. He played successive innings of 177 not out and 152 not out at Headingley and Lord's that exuded class, commitment and concentration. In particular he drove superbly through the covers, often with his back leg parallel to the ground. This strength off the front foot, and a certain jumpiness in defence off the back foot, led bowler after bowler to waste his energies in future years in trying to bounce him into submission. He decided to cut the hook shot from his repertoire but nimbleness, cussedness and infinite patience enabled him to win most of his battles with fast bowlers, not least the West Indian titans who alone got the better of Australia in most matches until the tables were turned at last in 1994-5. In that series Waugh averaged 107, and scored 200 in the final Test at Sabina Park that clinched the series.

Against England in 1997, his obdurate centuries in both innings turned the series towards Australia in a relatively low-scoring game. He remained a model of consistency in his years as captain, settling at number six in the batting order, a position from which he could play the game at the necessary pace. In 2001 he seriously pulled a calf muscle in the game in which Australia regained the Ashes at Trent Bridge and was written off for the rest of the series, but by sheer hard work and willpower got himself sufficiently fit to play the last game at the Oval and duly scored a century.

He retired on his own terms to a quieter life with his young family in 2004, having defied those who had wanted him to give up earlier by reaching an emotional century off the last ball of the day against England at Sydney in 2002-03.

62. BISHEN SINGH BEDI

Bishen Singh Bedi, b. 25 September 1946, Amritsar

First-class: 3,584 runs (11.37), 1,560 wickets (21.69) and 172 catches
Tests (67): 656 runs (8.98), 266 wickets (28.71) and 26 catches

Built, in his maturity, like one of the ox bullocks that were once a common sight pulling carts around the streets of India, Bishen Singh Bedi nevertheless moved to the wicket to bowl with all the lightness of a cloud. He was, perhaps, the subtlest master of slow left-arm flight since Wilfred Rhodes.

A devoted Sikh, instantly recognisable on any ground by his beard and colourful patkas, he prospered and held his own in an era when India was rich in spin-bowling talent. The equally flighty off-spinner Erapalli Prasana and the quicker, top-spinning Bhagwat Chandrasekhar were his chief accomplices.

An enigmatic character, quick to laugh and quick to ire, Bedi was a complete natural who made his debut for Northern Punjab in the Ranji Trophy at the age of fifteen. Once established in the Indian team, he played in 67 of the 75 Tests that were played during his international career. He adorned county cricket for Northamptonshire from 1972 to 1977, twice taking more than 100 wickets in a season.

He led India in 22 Tests from 1975 to 1976, always looking to win rather than draw. Only six matches were, in fact won, but he was always happy to bowl himself, not least when batsmen were looking to attack him, because few men have been so prepared to buy wickets so patiently.

He took 25 wickets in the losing series against England in 1976-77, starting with extraordinary figures of 86-43-109-5 at Delhi, and bowling 68.5 and 69 overs respectively in the first innings of the Bangalore and Bombay Tests.

Controversially, he twice declared India's innings closed at Sabina Park in 1975-76, when West Indies won by ten wickets and five of the Indian eleven were officially 'absent hurt' in the second innings. He was captain again when taking 31 wickets against Australia in 1977-78, including ten in the match at Perth.

Off the field, Bedi was – and remains – a man of strong views who enjoyed a drink and a friendly argument, a philosopher who has kept himself supple with yoga. On it, he was constantly exercising muscles and fingers to keep them loose for the supreme moment when he would come on to bowl, invariably to a tremendous cheer from a devoted public.

61. ARTHUR SHREWSBURY

Arthur Shrewsbury, b. 11 April 1856, New Lenton, Nottinghamshire; d. 19 May 1903, Gedling, Nottinghamshire

First-class: 26,505 runs (36.65) and 377 catches
Tests (23): 1,277 runs (35.47) and 29 catches

It is not just on 'Give me Arthur', W.G. Grace's famous response when asked who was the greatest batsman of his time, that Arthur Shrewsbury's reputation as a great player rests. For a significant period he was, in fact, a more productive batsman even than Grace himself, and C.B. Fry dismissed suggestions that he was no more than a great defensive player who relied on a somewhat pawky back-foot technique.

'He does not waste time and energy banging ball after ball into fieldsmen's hands,' said Fry: 'He waits and scores, waits and scores.' This was the way that all the best players did it until the one-day era demanded more calculated risk-taking: waiting for the bad ball and disposing of it efficiently. In his *Wisden* obituary Shrewsbury was described as being without an equal on sticky wickets. 'It was said of him that he seemed to see the ball closer up to the bat than any other player.'

Cricket quickly took precedence over his early training as an apprentice in the lace trade. Having played for Nottinghamshire's colts at the age of seventeen, for the county at nineteen and the Players at twenty, Shrewsbury played from the first, said Wisden, 'like one who had little to learn'. He went on to make more than 1,000 runs in thirteen seasons and to score ten double centuries.

A neat, precise figure who always wore a hat, he knew his worth. He would say to the attendant on the gate at Trent Bridge as he went out to bat, in the days before intervals: 'Bring me out a cup of tea at four o'clock.'

Despite Grace's official supremacy, Nottinghamshire's vigilant right-hander headed the first-class batting averages in England in five seasons between 1885 and 1892. His peak came in 1887 when he scored 1,653 runs at an average of 78, which was astounding for the times; but he missed the 1888 summer because he was busy managing a rugby team in Australia.

In common with the experience of the best professionals of his time, Australia became familiar to him. The sunshine brought the best out of him as a young batsman in 1881-82, and he led two sides comprising entirely professionals in the next few years. He averaged over 50 in 1884-85 and headed the batting averages on the tours of 1886-87 and the following year.

In all, Shrewsbury organised four tours of Australia as well as setting up a sports equipment firm with his business companions and fellow professionals Alfred Shaw and James Lillywhite. He and Shaw were the most prominent of the Nottinghamshire professionals who went on strike for fairer pay and more control over fixtures in 1881.

He became the first Test cricketer to score 1,000 runs and proved his greatness in several memorable innings, notably his 164 in the Lord's Test of 1886 when he resisted for nearly seven hours on a spiteful, drying pitch against, among others, Fred Spofforth, Hugh Trumble and George Giffen. On another 'unplayable' pitch at Lord's in 1893 he displayed similar mastery against C.T.B. Turner, scoring 106 and putting on 137 with F.S. Jackson.

A bachelor, he shot himself in 1903, believing himself, perhaps wrongly, to be suffering from an incurable kidney disease.

60. KEVIN PIETERSEN

Kevin Peter Pietersen, b. 27 June 1980, Pietermaritzburg

First-class: 10,705 runs (51.71), 61 wickets (52.85) and 110 catches
Tests (49): 4,333 runs (50.97), four wickets (128.25) and 30 catches
One-day internationals (87): 3,047 runs (48.36), five wickets and 31 catches

'I have three simple thoughts: play straight, play myself in and get to ten,' said Kevin Pietersen of his approach to batting soon after his brief elevation to the England captaincy in 2008. Notoriously a bad starter early in his career, as a county player for Nottinghamshire, he nevertheless made waves and headlines from the moment of his arrival. In fact, as well as in his own confident mind, once he reaches double figures he is usually bound for a big innings, which is not to

say that he has not given too many of them away when well set.

Once in control, however, Pietersen is demoralising for opponents and entertaining for spectators. A tall, powerful and very fit athlete, he plays shots that most batsmen cannot, dictates the terms with an air of supreme authority and is far more likely to get himself out through an excess of ambition than through the skill of opposing bowlers.

A young man in a hurry to be famous, he came to England determined to make his name as quickly as possible, qualifying for county cricket, though not yet for England, by virtue of his English mother. He had, he said, become frustrated by the South African quota system that allowed a set number of 'cricketers of colour' favoured advancement ahead of white ones in order to correct the social imbalances created by the apartheid system. He would still have come through there before long, because talent will out, but he soon made his mark as a nineteen-year-old for Nottinghamshire, scoring 1,275 first-class runs in his first county season, 2001. By 2005, after a move to Hampshire and a sensational start to his one-day international career in his native land the previous winter, he was ready for the next step.

Although there were suspicions amongst some that he was a 'flash Harry' – encouraged by camera-catching streaks in his hair, expensive earrings, a lucrative bat deal and a tattoo on his shoulders showing the England crown and three lions – the selectors rightly promoted him to the Test team for the Ashes series ahead of the still-effective stalwart Graham Thorpe.

He responded by making imposing fifties in both innings of his first Test at Lord's and then, on the final afternoon of a series that had had all Britain enthralled after Australia's long period of domination, produced a fusillade of powerful boundaries, including seven sixes, to ensure that the game would be drawn and the Ashes regained after the team had teetered on the brink of disaster. No one had hit so many sixes in an Anglo-Australia Test before as Pietersen in his 158. His six dropped catches in the series, purely the result of over-excitement, were forgotten.

An even more solid achievement followed in the next Ashes series in Australia, when he scored 490 runs at 54 in a badly mauled side that lost the series 0-5. At Adelaide in the second Test he scored 158, forcing the great Shane Warne to bowl defensively outside his legs from round the wicket. From that series he was England's key batsman, capable of producing an assiduously practised left-handed switch shot to swing a ball from Muttiah Muralitharan into the midst of an astonished crowd at Edgbaston, and of repeating it to counter Harbhajan Singh in India.

Time will tell whether the tall South African who replaced the weary Michael Vaughan as captain of his adopted country in 2008, only to relinquish the job five months later when the ECB forced his resignation after he had insisted on the removal of Peter Moores as head coach, will stand higher in the pantheon by the time that his career is complete. His early achievements and the independent nature of his approach to batting mark him as an exceptional talent possessed of the necessary character and determination. Already wealthy from cricketing and commercial endorsements, he signed for one of the eight franchises in the the Indian Premier League in 2009, for a salary over three years of $1.5 million US.

59. HEDLEY VERITY

Hedley Verity, b. 18 May 1905, Headingley, Leeds; d. 31 July 1943, Caserta, Italy

First-class: 5,605 runs (18.08), 1,956 wickets (14.90), and 268 catches
Tests (40): 669 runs (20.90), 144 wickets (24.37) and 30 catches

Although he was the successor of Wilfred Rhodes as the left-arm spinner in the Yorkshire and England side, Hedley Verity was in another sense the forerunner of Derek Underwood, a very accurate and intelligent purveyor of orthodox spin at a stock pace that was only a little short of medium. It may be hard for his contemporaries to envisage any bowler so natural, or so deadly on a drying pitch as Underwood,

but there is ample evidence that Verity's control was as good on true pitches, and his venom even more lethal on wet or drying ones.

Because of the perennial Rhodes it was not until he was 25 that he got into the Yorkshire side, and the Second World War ended both his career and his life. But in nine full seasons, at a time of great plenty for batsmen, he took an average of 180 wickets a season. In consecutive summers, 1935 to 1937, he took more than 200 wickets. Never in his nine full seasons was he below fifth in the national bowling averages.

These were days when the likes of Bradman, Ponsford and Woodfull were breaking run-scoring records in Australia and when Wally Hammond and at least ten others would routinely average more than 50 in the long season in England. But Verity's standards never dropped. He twice took all ten wickets in an innings – against Warwickshire at Headingley for 36 runs in 1931; and against Nottinghamshire the following season when he returned the famous analysis of ten for ten, also at Leeds. Against Essex at Leyton in 1933 he took seventeen in the match for 91 and, in his last game of first-class cricket, seven for nine against Sussex at Hove, in 1939.

In his seven years as an England regular he toured Australia, in 1932-33 and 1936-37, as well as South Africa, India and New Zealand. His most famous feat for England, fourteen wickets in one day on a drying pitch at Lord's in 1934, inspired England's only Test victory over Australia in the twentieth century. When he got on a sticky, his teammate Norman Yardley observed, he pushed the ball through on middle or middle-and-off without trying to spin it excessively.

Yet he enjoyed just as much his contests against Bradman and Hammond on good pitches and hot days. His teammate Bill Bowes wrote of his marvellous control of length and a direction, 'as straight as an arrow'. He also had a quicker arm ball. He would bowl it about sixteen times a season, Bowes said, 'and it would give him sixteen wickets'. He would make the ball lift on a wet wicket and bounce even on a dry one: 'Batsmen frequently found themselves playing the ball in the air when they thought they had got well over the top of it.'

Verity never flagged, wrote Terence Prittie, nor changed his appearance, whether he had just started to bowl or was labouring after hours under a hot sun:

His tread was the same, light and dancing, well on his toes, effortless and unbroken in its swift rhythm. His arm swung as freely as ever, came over as high as before in that smooth, well-rounded action which seemed to grow out of his run and melt back into it once more.

Dignified, undemonstrative, patient, determined and utterly reliable, Verity was in every sense well-rounded. He was a fine fielder off his own bowling or at backward point and made the most of his lesser ability as a batsman, to the extent that in 1936-37 he was promoted by the imaginative Gubby Allen to open for England in the Adelaide Test with Charlie Barnett. Their partnerships of 53 and 45 were the best for England in the five Tests.

Verity is a name that betokens honesty and steadfast faith. As Captain Verity of the Green Howards, he was badly wounded in battle on the Catania plain in Sicily in 1943. Captured by the Germans, he died three days after an operation in the military hospital at Caserta on the Italian mainland. His last words were: 'Keep going.'

58. KUMAR SANGAKKARA

Kumar Chokshanada Sangakkara, b. 27 October 1977, Matale, Sri Lanka

First-class: 11,148 runs (46.06), 314 catches and 33 stumpings
Tests (80): 6,764 runs (54.99), 153 catches and twenty stumpings
One-day internationals (246): 7,408 runs (36.31), 227 catches and 64 stumpings

The combination of piercing intelligence, intense competitiveness and a wealth of natural talent made a formidable all-round cricketer of Kumar Sangakkara, who has the potential to be a Sri Lankan C.B. Fry.

A scholar who writes and speaks well in Sinhalese, Tamil and English, he is the son of a leading lawyer in Kandy and was still working towards a legal qualification when the constant demands of international cricket intervened for a time.

Second only to Adam Gilchrist in world cricket as a wicket-keeper/batsman, he was asked to play only as a specialist batsman in Test cricket from 2007-08, while continuing both his roles in one-day cricket. He profited instantly from the decision. In nine Tests against five different opponents he scored seven centuries, three of them double hundreds, to become for a time the most highly rated batsman in the world.

A cultured left-hander batsman with quick reflexes, especially strong off the back foot on the off side, it was apparent that he was a player of high class as soon as he got into the one-day international side at the age of 22. His wicket-keeping lacked consistency at first, but never agility or slickness. What is more, he assailed batsmen from behind with persistent jabber, never afraid of retaliation, whether verbal or in the form of bouncers when he batted.

Having already made 232 against South Africa at the SSC ground in Colombo in 2004, he scored 287 there against the same opponents in 2007, sharing a record partnership of 624 with his friend and accomplice Mahela Jayawardena. That was followed by two centuries in a short series in New Zealand, and successive innings of 200 not out and 222 not out against Bangladesh. If the latter was like seizing a child's ice-cream there was nothing weak about the opposition in Australia, where Sangakkara made a flowing 192 in defeat at Hobart, or about a fresh and decent England attack at Kandy, where he followed up an innings of 92 out of 188 with a second-innings 152, a match-winning performance on his old school ground, Trinity College.

He had been robbed of a double hundred only by an umpiring error at Hobart. The century against England completed a full hand of hundreds against the other nine Test countries and was his fourth score of 150 or more in consecutive Tests, a record. By the end of that series, Sangakkara had taken his Test average to 83.05 for the games in which he had not kept wicket.

57. JAVED MIANDAD

Javed Miandad Khan, b. 12 June 1937, Karachi, Pakistan

First-class: 28,663 runs (53.37), 191 wickets (33.48), 341 catches and
three stumpings
Tests (124): 8832 runs (52.57), seventeen wickets (40.11), 93 catches and
one stumping
One-day internationals (233): 7,381 (41.70), seven wickets (42.42), 71
catches and two stumpings

Controversial and commercial though he may have been, Javed Miandad was a genius of a batsman who played the ball exceptionally late and worked it about the field with flexible wrists, like a squash player manipulating the rubber ball round a court. For talent alone there have been very few to match him.

Despite his huge pile of runs, he was far from being one of those patient accumulators who like to go on and on. Quite often he would get himself out through over-confidence or ambition. At 92 not out against Sri Lanka in 1981-82, for example, with the bowling at his mercy, he spotted out of the corner of his eye that mid-off was still walking back to his mark with his back turned as the leg-spinner, D.S. de Silva, was running in to bowl. Dancing out to try to lift the ball over the errant fielder's head, he was stumped instead.

Javed was one of five Miandad brothers who learned the game at the Muslim Gymkhana Club in Karachi, where his father had become the secretary after Partition. He was not, therefore, quite the street fighter that he appeared to be when batting for Pakistan, but it seemed to come naturally to him to niggle the opposition. He had a furious public row with Dennis Lillee in Australia in 1981-82, delighted in stirring the pot after the row between the England captain Mike Gatting and the umpire Shakoor Rana at Faisalabad in 1987-88, and

as captain again in England in 1992 he managed to rile both umpires and opposition.

There was a mischievous look about him that suggested that for him this was all part of the game. There was sometimes a wider game too. He twice resigned the Test captaincy only to reclaim it and, when he retired, twice also resigned as Pakistan's chief coach, only to be given the reins again in 2008 in a period of familiar upheaval. In all he captained Pakistan in 54 Tests, winning fourteen of them and losing only six. He also played in 53 successive Tests between December 1977 and January 1984.

He was so good so young that he made a maiden first-class appearance at the age of sixteen, and scored 311 for Karachi Whites against National Bank at seventeen and a double century in his third Test at nineteen. New Zealand, his hapless opponents in 1976-77, had already seen the teenager make a commanding 163 in his first Test innings at Lahore. In 1978-79 he scored four more centuries, two at home to India and one each on tour of Australia, on the fast pitch at Perth, and in New Zealand.

He could play well on any sort of pitch, as his prolific performances in county cricket for Sussex and Glamorgan showed, but at home on the slow, grassless ones he broke even more bowlers' hearts. He scored 280 not out against India at Hyderabad in Sind in 1981-82, and on the same ground three years later made two hundreds in the same game against New Zealand. His remorseless 260 against England at the Oval in 1987 assured Pakistan of the series.

All the while he was also a brilliant one-day cricketer. Early in his career his leg spin was accurate enough to get through twelve overs of leg-spin in the first World Cup in England against the eventual winners, West Indies, in 1975. Seventeen years later, in Melbourne, he played the innings that rescued Pakistan sufficiently for them to win the final against England.

56. LEARIE CONSTANTINE

Baron Sir Learie Nicholas Constantine, b. Diego Martin, Trinidad

First-class: 4,475 runs (24.05), 439 wickets (20.48) and 133 catches
Tests (18): 635 runs (19.24), 58 wickets (30.10) and 28 catches

Figures cannot convey the joyous talent of Learie Constantine, the grandson of a slave, who started life humbly in Port of Spain and finished it in England as Baron Constantine of Maraval and Nelson, an inspiration and example to the post-war immigrants to England from the Caribbean.

His father, Lebrun, was the most popular cricketer in Trinidad, went to England in 1900 with the first West Indies team, his passage paid for by public subscription, and scored the first hundred on the tour. He scored 1,000 runs when he came again in 1906. He also kept wicket and took 46 first-class wickets at thirteen each. At home he would hit high catches to young Learie and his brother Elias until the short twilight had become darkness on the plantation at Diego Martin. Elias also played for Trinidad, and Lebrun and Learie played together in the old man's last match for the island.

Long-armed and beady-eyed, Learie became the greatest fielder of his time, a feline, loose-limbed marvel in the covers or a close fielder who brought off catches that no one else could have reached. In addition he was a dangerous, unorthodox, magnetic attacking batsman who scored 78 out of 103 in 55 minutes on the last day of the 1939 Test at the Oval, and an uninhibited fast bowler in his youth with a bounding approach who became an extremely canny medium-paced one later. In the same Oval Test in 1939, he took five for 75 in the first innings on a perfect pitch.

His lasting fame on the cricket field rested largely on one amazing season in England in 1928, when his fielding was at its zenith and he held no fewer than 33 catches. It was his only full season in first-class

cricket and he did the double. Against Middlesex at Lord's he scored 86 in half an hour in the first innings to rescue the touring team from 79 for five, then took seven for 57. Set 259 to win, the West Indians were 121 for five before he hit 103 out of 133 in an hour, with two sixes and twelve fours, to win the game. On the tour he took 107 wickets at 22 and made 1,381 runs.

He was a great disappointment in the three Tests, but made up for it to an extent at home in 1929-30 when his eighteen wickets included nine for 122 at Georgetown in the first-ever West Indies win over England. On their first tour of Australia in 1930-31 his 47 wickets came at only twenty each and his 708 runs at an average of 30. By now he had become the biggest attraction in the Lancashire league, playing for Nelson in an area where he was to spend much of his life. In 1934-35, his 90 at Port of Spain and three for eleven in fourteen overs in the second innings led to another victory over England, and he took fifteen wickets at only thirteen each in the series.

Surely, said Raymond Robertson-Glasgow, 'no man ever gave or received more joy by the mere playing of cricket'. There was intelligence as well as joie de vivre in his cricket, and he used both when he had stopped playing. He became prominent in welfare work in England during the war, was called to the Bar, became Minister of Works in the Trinidadian government and High Commissioner to London.

55. ALLAN BORDER

Allan Robert Border, b. 27 July 1955, Sydney

First-class: 27,131 runs (51.38), 106 wickets (39.25) and 379 catches
Tests (156): 11,174 runs (50.56), 39 wickets (39.10) and 156 catches
One-day internationals (273): 6,524 runs (30.62), 73 wickets (28.36) and 127 catches

Allan Border's unequalled doggedness brings to mind the lines of W.E. Henley: 'Out of the night that covers me, black as the pit from pole to pole, I thank whatever Gods may be, for my unconquerable soul.' No night seemed too black for Border. He might and could have been an extremely attractive, even dashing left-handed batsman, but at a time of trial he made himself into one ruled by an iron discipline. By sheer willpower he inspired a lasting recovery in his country's cricketing fortunes.

As his career ground remorselessly on, Test after Test followed by one-day international after one-day international, his resolve seemed only to get deeper. Having first bettered then buried 'the Poms', who had been the superior team in his early days as an international, he set about defying the fast bowlers of the West Indies. The teams he led never quite got the better of them, but by the time that the reins were finally taken from him – he was certainly never going to let them go voluntarily – the days of vengeance were not far off. By then Border was a national treasure. Every Aussie knew whom another was talking about when he spoke of 'A.B.' and they still do. Like the 'Don' and the racehorse Phar Leap, he has passed into Aussie sporting legend.

Having made his mark for his Sydney club, Mosman, and briefly for New South Wales, he was picked for Australia sooner than he would have been had senior players not been otherwise engaged with World Series Cricket. A stocky left-hander with a sound technique, ruthless as a cutter and puller of the short ball, he was a useful left-arm orthodox slow bowler, a fine close catcher and, in one-day cricket at mid-wicket especially, a deadly thrower, helped by skills learned from playing baseball in his youth.

He showed flair as well as defiance in scoring 60 not out and 45 not out in his second Test in defeat against England on a turning pitch at Sydney in 1978-79, made a maiden Test century against Pakistan later that season, and in six Tests in India at the start of the 1978-79 season scored 521 runs. He retained his place when the World Series Cricket players returned, playing at home against England and the West Indies before returning to the subcontinent to score 150 not out and 153 not out in the same Test at Lahore. He went on to play 153 consecutive Test matches, leading Australia in 93 of them and going on 28 tours.

Easily Australia's leading batsman in England in 1981, with 533 runs at 59, he scored 123 not out in the second innings at Old Trafford despite batting throughout with a broken finger. The same raw courage was evident in the Caribbean early in 1984 when he scored 521 Test runs at 74, dodging the bouncers with unblinking eyes. After another Ashes reverse in 1985 he spent two highly productive seasons for Essex in 1986 and 1988, scoring more than 1,000 runs both times.

Beating England in the World Cup final in Calcutta seemed to kick-start the longed-for revival. His early days as Australia's captain, after the simultaneous loss of three senior players – Lillee, Marsh and Greg Chappell – and the resignation of Kim Hughes in November 1984, were wretched. Australia went seven series without winning one and Border, often tetchy with the press and his own players, not to mention opponents, acquired the nickname 'Captain Grumpy'. The appointment of Bobby Simpson as coach took some of the weight off him and also added battle-hardened wisdom. When he returned to England in 1989 Border, once a drinking partner of Ian Botham's but now advised to cut out any fraternising with opponents by another tough captain, Ian Chappell, had a carapace that became harder and harder.

Having lost thirteen and won only six Tests under his captaincy before 1988, Australia won sixteen and lost only three over the next four years. By the time that the Ashes had been won easily again at home and away, with men such as the Waugh brothers, Mark Taylor, David Boon, Michael Slater, Ian Healy, Merv Hughes and, above all, Shane Warne in the side, the base had been laid for taking over the supremacy of world cricket from the West Indies. Border scored 200 not out at Leeds in his last Ashes series, and even when he lost the captaincy against his will played on to help Queensland win the Sheffield Shield for the first time.

He remains closely connected with cricket, and the Allan Border Oval at Brisbane houses an Australian Cricket Academy.

54. CLARRIE GRIMMETT

Clarence Victor Grimmett, b. 24 December 1891, Dunedin; d. 2 May 1980, Adelaide

First-class: 4,720 runs (17.67), 1,424 wickets (22. 28) and 139 catches
Tests (37): 557 runs (13. 93), 216 wickets (24.22) and seventeen catches

New Zealand's greatest gift to Australian cricket, Clarrie Grimmett may have looked like a garden gnome but his wizardry conjured up 216 wickets in only 37 Tests. He was the other half of wrist-spin partnerships with Arthur Mailey and Bill O'Reilly that kept Australia generally on top of opponents between 1925 and 1936, although, especially against some strong England sides, it was only when Don Bradman gave the leg-spinners so many runs to play with that victories became commonplace.

Grimmett was a leg-spinning boffin, so closely did he study and work at the art. One can almost imagine him doing experiments with test tubes at his home in Adelaide. His family migrated in 1914, when he had already played nine games for his native Wellington, and he moved to his eventual home in South Australia via Sydney and Melbourne, where he practised bowling for hours on end in his garden, having trained his fox terrier, Joe, to fetch the balls for him from an empty net.

It took time for his skill to be appreciated, no doubt because of the oddness of his action, which had none of the classical perfection of later experts such as Richie Benaud and Bruce Dooland. He began with a little skip, came in diagonally and, as Ian Peebles, another more classical exponent, phrased it, 'swung a bony arm a little above shoulder high'. He bowled leg breaks across a range of subtly varied speeds, mixed them with a quite easily spotted googly, which he used for tactical variation, and also with a deadly, dipping top spinner. In addition he invented the flipper, the product of hours of profound study and constant practice.

His accuracy was phenomenal by the time that he accepted a job as cricketer and sign-writer at the Adelaide Cricket Club in 1924 and he took eight for 86 in his first match for South Australia against Victoria, whose selectors had picked him for only five matches in six seasons. By the end of that season he was in the Test side at the age of 34, and not before time. He took five for 45 and six for 37 in his first Test at Sydney. England, bamboozled and bowled out for 167 and 146, lost heavily.

When he went to England for the first time in 1926, he turned the ball more than he had at home and took more than 100 wickets. In 1930 he took all ten wickets in an innings against Yorkshire at Sheffield and 29 in the Tests; in 1934 another 28 in the series. With O'Reilly he shared 169 wickets in their fifteen Tests in tandem, against England and South Africa. Grimmett took 88 of them, finishing with 44 at 14.59 each in his final series in South Africa. He was then dropped prematurely but, despite his late start, finished with 129 more Sheffield Shield wickets – 513 – than his nearest rival before or since, Terry Alderman.

53. GEOFFREY BOYCOTT

Geoffrey Boycott, b. 21 October 1940, Fitzwilliam, Yorkshire

First-class: 48,426 runs (56.83), 45 wickets (32.42) and 264 catches
Tests (108): 8,114 runs (47.72), seven wickets (54.57) and seven catches
One-day internationals (36): 1,082 runs (36.06), five wickets (21.00) and five catches

There is a bronze sculpture of the on-drive off Greg Chappell with which Geoffrey Boycott reached his 100th first-class hundred in the perfect context, against Australia in a Test match for England on his home ground at Headingley. It was the high point of an extraordinary career.

No cricketer has divided opinion so often or so fiercely, especially in his native Yorkshire, but of the technical expertise and shrewd application of his batting there is no doubt. He was one of the great opening batsmen and a professional whose single-minded pursuit of excellence, to the exclusion of all else for much of his career, has not been equalled.

Stubborn, opinionated and determined to look after himself in a world that seemed to him to be against him, he ploughed a lonely furrow through a long career. His cricket was deeply respected by all against whom he played, though many of them did not much take to his obduracy. His teammates knew him as a singular man who would always prefer to be in a net than a bar. Very few got close to him, and one or two vehemently disliked him for what they perceived as selfishness. But they all knew that no one was better equipped to go out to face fast bowling, either for Yorkshire or for England.

Boycott, from a mining family near Wakefield, had to struggle to get into the Yorkshire side, which may account for his rare inner drive.

Once there, he rapidly established his ability and was playing for England two years later, although he was only laying the base for his mountain of runs. Right-handed, five foot ten inches and with a wiry strength, he was an especially productive player square on the off side but he played all the strokes when he felt that he could safely do so.

That he usually restrained his natural talent was evident from the exceptional display of free-spirited stroke play in the 1965 Gillette Cup final when, following a season in which for once he had not scored a first-class century, he unleashed his potential to make 146 with three sixes and fifteen fours to inspire a Yorkshire side with eleven Test players to an easy victory over Surrey.

Yorkshire's ascendancy did not last, but Boycott's did. In Australia his 657 runs in five Tests at an average of 93 was a key element in England's regaining of the Ashes. The following season, 1971, his first as Yorkshire's captain, he scored 2,503 runs to become the first English player to average 100 in a season in England, but Yorkshire still went seventeen matches without winning. They were never to win

a title under his command, despite another fine season in 1979 when again he averaged 100.

Caring as much for his county as his country, and disappointed not to be made England captain after Ray Illingworth, he exiled himself from the national side for three years from 1974, missing 30 Tests. He returned to make successive scores of 107, 80 not out and 191 in 1977 to help England to regain the Ashes. He led England in four Tests overseas in 1977-78 while Mike Brearley was injured.

He played one of his finest innings in tricky conditions against Australia, 137 at the Oval in 1981, and the following winter a century at Delhi made him, for a time, the highest scorer in Test cricket. But he seemed to lose interest after that; he was sent home early, officially because he was unwell, and appeared a few weeks later as the senior batsman on a disapproved tour in South Africa. Banned from international cricket for two years along with fourteen other players he continued to score heavily in domestic cricket, reaching 100 hundreds for Yorkshire alone in 1985. At the age of 45 he averaged 52 in his last season, overtaking Herbert Sutcliffe's record of 149 Yorkshire hundreds. Seven of his ten double hundreds were for Yorkshire, and he made more than 1,000 runs in 23 home seasons.

Curiously for one so tough, he was a woman's man who found solace in several close relationships, one of which ended bitterly in a French courtroom. Generally, although he was the cause of constant fighting among Yorkshire cricket club members, the public loved him for his wonderful reliability as a batsman. His success and acquisitiveness enabled him to accumulate considerable wealth, helped by a generous bequest from an admiring widow. He became a successful and widely travelled pundit on the game for radio and television, a shrewd judge who gave his views trenchantly but fairly.

52. JACQUES KALLIS

Jacques Henry Kallis, b. 16 October 1975, Cape Town

First-class: 16,412 runs (53.28), 390 wickets (30.41) and 206 catches
Tests (129): 10,060 runs (54.37), 255 wickets (30.97) and 144 catches
One-day internationals (287): 10,057 runs (45.30), 246 wickets (31.72)
and 105 catches

An all-round cricketer of exalted class, Jacques Kallis needed only charisma, and sometimes a little more urgency in his batting when the situation demanded, to be mentioned in the same breath as the likes of Walter Hammond and Garfield Sobers.

A tall, massively strong man, his talent was being talked about in Cape Town in awed tones even before he was picked for Western Province and then, in 1995-96, for South Africa. He rapidly established himself as a batsman with a superb technique and calm temperament who seemed always to have seconds more time to see the ball and to get into position to play it than anyone else.

As a fast-medium bowler with a classical sideways-on action who could be genuinely quick, he had all the attributes to have succeeded at the top level in that role alone, swinging the ball with both the old ball and, when occasionally he gets it, the new one. His fielding is top-class, especially in the slips, and at the wicket he bats with the air of one who can ride above any storm. His expression never changes, whether he has just nodded his head out of the path of a bouncer or stroked a four through extra cover after a large forward stride and the seemingly effortless placement of a broad-looking bat into the path of the ball.

There have been political and social storms to ride in his career too, not to mention the scandal involving his first international captain, Hansie Cronje. A decent and dignified man, Kallis steered clear of trouble, kept his own counsel and concentrated on developing his cricket with utter professionalism. His right to a place in the South Africa side was never questioned, and by April 2006 he had played 100 Test matches and more than 200 one-day internationals.

There has been no flagging since. His record shows extraordinary stamina both mentally and physically, because his has been the wicket that opponents most wanted. Some relatively sluggish innings during the 2007 World Cup, however, led to his omission from the first World

Twenty20 competition on his own territory later that year. Twenty20 requires unorthodoxy and risk-taking that do not come easily to Kallis but, as if to prove he could dominate in any circumstances, he took complete charge of a useful Pakistan attack on the tour that soon followed, scoring 155 and 100 not out in the first Test at Karachi and 59 and 107 not out in the second at Lahore. In nine Tests in 2007 he scored 1,210 runs at 86 and took twenty wickets at 25.

Starting with an innings of 101 against Australia at Melbourne in 1997-98, this implacable and insatiable cricketer had run up 30 Test centuries by 2008, few of them memorable but each made with such unhurried composure that opposing bowlers could have seen the writing on the wall long before they were reached.

51. CURTLY AMBROSE

Curtly Elconn Lynwall Ambrose, b. 21 September 1963, Swetes Village, Antigua

First-class: 3,448 runs (13.95), 941 wickets (20.24) and 88 catches
Tests (98): 1,439 runs (12.40); 405 wickets (20.99) and eighteen catches
One-day internationals (176): 639 runs (10.65), 225 wickets (24.13) and
45 catches

In a line of tall, forbiddingly fast and accurate bowlers that started with the demon Spofforth, Curtly Elconn Lynwall Ambrose – his third name inspired by Ray Lindwall – sustained the tradition of fast-bowling prowess that made the West Indies the best team in the world throughout his career. Six foot seven inches tall and thin as a rake, he maintained his form remarkably well through a tough programme of international matches, sharing a fearsome new-ball partnership with another giant, the broader and stronger-looking Jamaican Courtney Walsh.

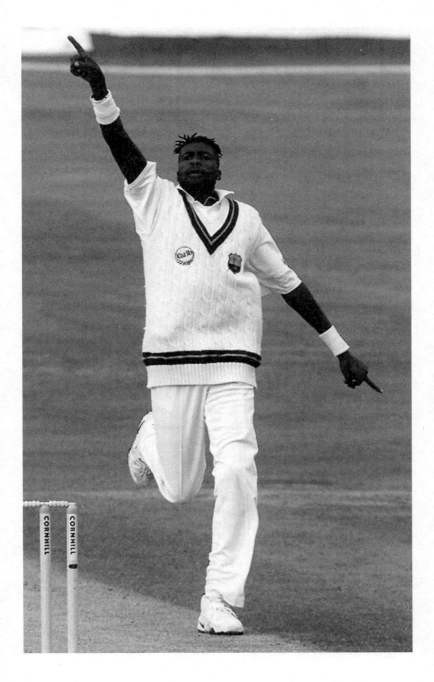

A country boy from Swetes village in Antigua, he had to be persuaded to take up cricket by a cricket-mad mother who would ring a bell outside her home whenever he took a wicket as she watched on television. He had shown little interest in the game as a boy but bowling came naturally, by imitation rather than by any coaching. Nor was he by any means a rabbit with the bat.

'Curtly' – the cricket world knew him as that without need for the surname – has always had a smile as wide as a sliced melon when he is relaxing off the field. He became a guitar-playing member of a band when he retired, sharing the stage with the former West Indies captain, Richie Richardson, but there were no smiles when he was bowling. Loose-limbed and rhythmical, he bounded to the crease like an elongated kangaroo, a straight run-up culminating in a high, repeating action which delivered steepling bounce and great pace. It was an oddity of his action that his loose right wrist would wave the ball towards the batsman in the instant before he entered his delivery stride.

Like the Barbadian giant Joel Garner, who was an inch taller, Curtly possessed a wicked yorker, a nasty bouncer and the ability to make batsmen go back because of the bounce he got from a good length. Twenty-four per cent of his Test victims were caught by the wicket-keeper, 20 per cent bowled and 13 per cent LBW. He was like a giant shadow forever hovering over his opponents and, sooner or later, he hounded most of them into submission. He had great stamina, missing only one of the 49 Tests played by the West Indies after his first appearance, and that not because of the usual fast-bowling problems with back or knees but because of haemorrhoids.

Having pondered emigration to the USA to try his luck at basketball, he came to cricket relatively late, learning his trade by playing league cricket in Lancashire before bursting onto the Caribbean scene in the 1988 Red Stripe tournament. He took 35 wickets at fifteen and was soon a Test player. His first visits to England and Australia produced figures, respectively, of 22 wickets at twenty and 26 at 21.

At home against England, an upset still seemed possible after England's win in the first Test in Kingston in 1990 when Ambrose demolished his opponents at Bridgetown with a ruthless new-ball spell of five for eighteen on the final evening of the match. He finished with figures of eight for 45. If anything, he was even more devastating at the Queen's Park Oval in Trinidad in 1994 when he made a mockery of England's modest victory target of 194 by taking six for 22 in 7.5 overs as his demoralised opponents collapsed to 40 for eight on the fourth evening of the third Test.

There were two other legendary spells: six for 34 in the second innings of South Africa's first Test against the West Indies to win the game at Bridgetown; and seven for one in 32 balls against Australia at Perth in 1993. That was also the scene of his greatest embarrassment. In the final Test of the 1996-97 series against Australia, he bowled a fifteen-ball over that contained nine no-balls and took twelve minutes to bowl.

50. GEORGE LOHMANN

George Alfred Lohmann, b. 2 June 1865, Kensington, London; d. 1 December 1901, Matjiesfontein, Karoo, South Africa

First-class: 7,247 runs (18.68), 1,805 wickets (13.91) and 334 catches
Tests (18): 213 runs (8.87), 112 wickets (10.75) and 28 catches

George Lohmann's was a short career in a sadly short life, but what he achieved in cricket before tuberculosis killed him at the age of 36 was fabled, unprecedented and in one respect unsurpassed. As a match-winning bowler, the first of the great medium-pacers, he had a better average and wicket-striking rate in Test cricket than any man before or since.

The broad-shouldered, blond-haired, blue-eyed son of a London stockbroker's clerk, he learned his cricket on Wandsworth Common in south London, playing for his local Church Institute. He excelled

at once, was spotted as a teenager bowling to a friend in the nets at the Oval and was taken on by Surrey in 1884.

He was a bold, attacking batsman, a genius of a slip fielder and a bowler whom both W.G. Grace and C.B. Fry rated as the finest exponent of medium pace they had ever seen. The forerunner of Sydney Barnes, he had complete control, clever variations of pace and the ability to spin and cut the ball at will. To his ultimate cost, he was also tireless until burning himself out after a mere ten years at the top.

The pillar of Surrey's Championship-winning sides in the late 1880s and early 1890s, he took 200 wickets three seasons in a row from 1888 to 1890. He toured Australia three times and South Africa in 1895-96, where again he foreshadowed Barnes by dominating on the matting pitches with 35 wickets at a cost of only 5.80 runs each in three Tests. At Port Elizabeth his figures were seven for 38 and eight for seven. Among other astonishing performances, he took seven for 36 against Australia at the Oval in 1886, eight for 25 at Sydney in 1886-87 and eight for 58 on the same ground on the last of his three tours there in 1891-92.

There was more to Lohmann than winning matches. He came from a middle-class background and knew his social and professional worth. With four others picked to play for England at the Oval in 1886, for a fee of £10 that had been unchanged since 1880, he wrote to the Surrey committee asking for £20. The issue had been brewing all summer but the response was a terse telegram to the Surrey dressing-room at Leyton, where they were playing Essex: 'Fee for playing England v. Australia £10 or you are out of the match.' Three of the players gave way but Lohmann and William Gunn of Nottinghamshire did not. Two years later Test fees were, indeed, increased to £20.

Lohmann's health had first broken down in 1892 and he was advised to go to South Africa to recover. It became his winter home and he played a major role in the development of the game there as a coach and administrator.

49. HAROLD LARWOOD

Harold Larwood, born 14 November 1904, Nuncargate, Nottinghamshire; d. 22 July 1995, Sydney

First-class: 7,290 runs (19.91), 1,427 wickets (17.51) and 234 catches
Tests (28): 485 runs (19.40), 78 wickets (28.35) and fifteen catches

Truly exceptional pace and absolute accuracy are a rare combination. For a few years, and in one dramatic Australian season in particular, Harold Larwood possessed both. Thereby he became the main weapon in England's regaining the Ashes under Douglas Jardine's leadership in 1932-33 and the means by which, for a brief period, they managed to bring Don Bradman down almost to the same level as the other batsmen.

Those who saw Larwood at close hand in 1933 believed that no man could ever have bowled faster. No more than medium height for the era, and small by present standards for a fast bowler, he was broad-shouldered, strong and had long arms. He ran in eighteen yards with smooth acceleration and the delivery was perfectly coordinated. Jardine, among others, noticed that at full pace the final swing of his right arm would begin at the height of his calf and finish with his fingers actually brushing the ground in his follow-through. In Australia his skiddy, relatively low-trajectory bounce was all the more lethal.

First appearing for Nottinghamshire in 1924 he played for England two seasons later, taking three wickets in each innings of the Oval Test. In 1928-29 he started the next Ashes series with first innings figures of six for 32, having shown his batting ability at number nine in the order with a hard-hit 70. Lifeless pitches at home in 1930 neutered his pace except at the Oval where for a time, after rain, he had Bradman visibly apprehensive and struck him in the chest.

For Larwood himself the triumph that followed in Australia in 1932-33 was a mixed blessing. A hero at the time for bowling like the

wind in game after game, it was he who mainly reaped the whirlwind of reproach, initially from Australia but later in England too, as the implications of the 'bodyline' tactics that he had applied with such simple efficiency began to touch the consciences of more sensitive souls than Jardine.

Intensely loyal to his austere captain, Larwood had merely bowled according to the strategy that had been laid down, which included liberal doses of short-pitched balls lifting towards the ribs, with a semi-circle of short-leg fieldsmen to catch the edges and others posted further back for batsmen attempting to counter-attack. Only Stan McCabe, a brilliant hooker, and Bradman, by drawing away to leg to cut and carve through the off-side, came up with much of an answer.

Larwood was 29 when the tour ended but he did not play for England again, having taken 33 wickets at 19.51 in the series and finished it with a personal triumph, an innings of 98 in the Sydney Test for which he received a standing ovation despite the hostility shown to him by the crowds earlier in the series. There were three reasons, the first being physical. He had seriously damaged his left foot by hammering it down on the hard grounds of Australia. He went home early and missed the New Zealand leg of the trip. He did not have an operation until 1934, when the Australians were in England and he took 82 wickets, despite having lost his sharpest edge.

He was not helped by the need, clearly perceived in the MCC committee room, to mend fences with the Australians; nor by his own intransigence. Even as he arrived in England, encouraged by the Nottinghamshire captain Arthur Carr, he was unwisely putting his name to a series of newspaper articles – and to a quickly-published book – that stirred up the old indignation in Australia. Told by the wealthy Nottinghamshire patron Julian Cahn that he would have to apologise before playing against Australia again in 1934, he refused. In the *Sunday Dispatch* on 17 June Larwood announced that he had made up his mind 'not to play against the Australians in this or any of the Tests'.

A further 119 wickets at 12.97 in 1936, however, suggested that, even as a fast-medium bowler off a shorter run he would certainly have been picked again in normal circumstances. Harold Larwood really should have been even more celebrated than he was in retirement, although he and Bill Voce, his opening partner for Nottinghamshire and England, received a standing ovation when they walked to the middle at Trent Bridge during a lunch interval as guests at a Nottingham Test many years after their halcyon days, Larwood dwarfed by his broad-shouldered mate.

In 1950 he emigrated to Australia with his wife and five daughters. Curiously enough a similarly explosive fast bowler, Frank Tyson, did the same a few years after his 1954-55 triumph. I visited Larwood at his bungalow in Sydney in the 1970s. He was charming, modest and uncomplaining, much loved in his own home and as contented as anyone could be living in a Sydney suburb with his heart still in Nottingham. The silver ashtray presented to him by Jardine – 'To Harold for the Ashes, 1932-33 – from a grateful Skipper' – had pride of place on his mantelpiece.

48. KAPIL DEV

Kapil Dev Ramlal Nikhanj, b. 6 January 1959, Chandigarh

First-class: 11,356 runs (32.91), 835 wickets (27.09) and 192 catches
Tests (131): 5,248 runs (31.05), 434 wickets (29.64) and 64 catches
One-day internationals (225): 3,783 runs (23.79), 253 wickets (27.45)
and 71 catches

At the Oval in the final Test of 1982, Kapil Dev came out to bat when India needed 147 to avoid a follow-on against England with five wickets left. With strokes of pristine precision he hit 97 of 92 balls in 102 minutes. Eight years later, at Lord's, the ninth Indian wicket fell when his side still needed 24 to avoid another possible follow-on. Kapil's response this time was to drive the off-spinner straight back over his head for four successive sixes to the Nursery end. This was typical of

one of the most dynamic all-round cricketers international cricket has seen, and the most charismatic player to emerge from India since Prince Ranjitsinhji.

Kapil himself played the game like a prince, with a proud bearing and an air of command, whether or not he was captain and no matter what the situation. He was a strong, handsome six-footer with a vivid bowling action that culminated in a leap with the eyes looking classically over his left shoulder at the waiting batsman. He always swung the new ball and despite getting little help from his own pitches, he took his 434 Test wickets at 29.64, a phenomenal reward for his fitness, stamina and determination. A fine, athletic fieldsman and fierce driver, possessed of every shot in the book, he scored his runs, more often than not, with élan.

Kapil became known as the 'Haryana Hurricane', but this was not quite appropriate because out-and-out pace was not his main weapon. He was simply quick and accurate enough to make his swing count. He came from Chandigarh on the borders of Haryana and the Punjab, his parents having opted for India rather than Pakistan at Partition in 1947 although they had lived near Rawalpindi. Had they stayed, as Scyld Berry observed, he might have opened the bowling for Pakistan with Imran Khan.

Some startling analyses for Haryana as a teenager, starting with six for 39 in his first Ranji trophy match against Punjab, hurried him into the Test team against Pakistan in 1978-79. At first the adamantine pitches restricted his success, but against the West Indies he took seven for 84 in the match, and with 329 runs in the series at an average of 65.8 he was on his way. Twenty-eight wickets at 22 against Australia, and 32 at only seventeen against Pakistan in home series in 1978-79, helped him to reach the Test double of 1,000 runs and 100 wickets in just 25 matches, fewer than any save Mankad and Botham.

Succeeding Sunil Gavaskar as captain after a heavy defeat for India in Pakistan – unforgivable, apparently – he was unable to turn the tide in the West Indies, but in England in 1983 he led from the front to enable India to pull off an unexpected triumph in the third Prudential World Cup, which not only enhanced the fame and wealth of Kapil overnight but fundamentally changed the priorities of Indian cricket forever. After they had defeated the West Indies in the final at

Lord's, one-day international cricket became their chief focus. It might not have happened had Kapil not saved his side in an earlier match at Tunbridge Wells, when Zimbabwe had reduced his side to 20 for four and 78 for seven before Kapil, nothing daunted, blazed his way to 175 not out.

Many of his greatest battles thereafter, other than frequent arguments about whether he should be captain (he lost the job to his rival Gavaskar and then regained it) were with the West Indies, much the best team of the era. Yet he took nine for 83 against them at Ahmedabad in 1983-84 and 29 wickets in the series at 18.5. Intensive cricket inevitably took the edge off his bowling, but he soldiered on to produce the extraordinary double of 5,000 Test runs and 400 wickets.

Involved partly in cricket, partly in business on his retirement, he combined the two by playing a leading role in founding the Indian Cricket League, thus becoming embroiled in a bitter internecine war with the rival Indian Premier League, which enjoyed official support from the Board of Control for Cricket in India. Kapil had never been afraid of a fight.

47. RICKY PONTING

Ricky Thomas Ponting, b. 19 December 1974, Launceston, Tasmania

First-class: 19,689 runs (59.12), fourteen wickets (54.85) and 232 catches
Tests (129): 10,858 runs (56.84), five wickets (48.40) and 144 catches
One-day internationals (310): 11,365 runs (42.72), three wickets (34.66)
and 137 catches

The nickname 'Punter' stuck with Ricky Ponting long after he had conquered the occasional excess at the bookies' or in the bar. A superbly fit and totally dedicated model professional he may have

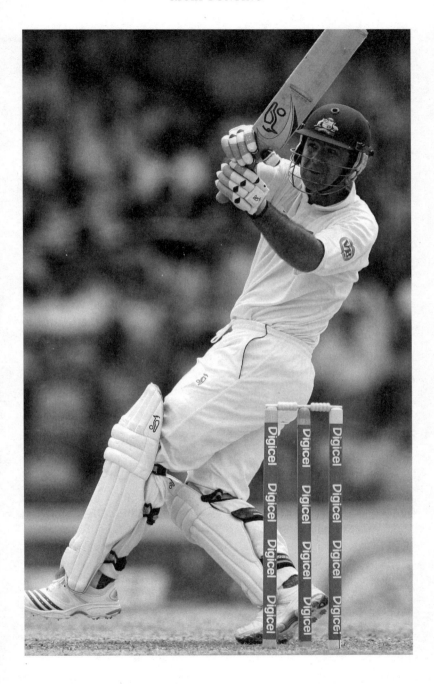

become, but there was no taking the 'punter' out of Ponting as a bats-man. Throughout his career he has backed himself against any bowler and only one, Harbhajan Singh, can claim consistently to have got the better of him.

Ponting learned his cricket at Launceston in Tasmania. When he was eight he was given a T-shirt by his grandmother bearing the words: 'Under this shirt is a Test player.' A little, dark-eyed batsman in the long tradition of quick-footed and aggressive Australians – it stretches to Ponting through such players as Charlie Macartney, Don Bradman and Lindsay Hassett – he is a brilliant fielder and has been one of the five best batsmen in the world through most of his time as captain of Australia. It started in 2002, when he took on the one-day leadership from Steve Waugh. Under his command his teams swept to dominating victories in the World Cup finals of 2003 in South Africa and 2007 in the Caribbean. In the first of them, at Johannesburg, he took command of the game with a dazzling innings of 140 from 121 balls, hitting eight sixes in his last 47 balls.

His tenacity under fire is very much part of the same tradition. He responded to unexpected defeat in England in 2005, despite his match-saving 156 at Old Trafford, by leading his side to sixteen successive victories and nineteen out of twenty, including the 5-0 win in the Ashes series of 2006-07. His was the best Australia side since the previous whitewash, in 1921. Typically, Ponting set the trend for the coolly calculated revenge against England by scoring 196 in the first Test at Brisbane. It repeated his hundred on the same ground in the previous home series after Nasser Hussain had put Australia into bat.

Such performances were the mark of a truly great batsman, one who could prepare for a big occasion and virtually guarantee adorn-ing it with an outstanding innings. He marked his 100th Test, against South Africa at Sydney in 2006, by scoring a century in each innings.

As was the case under Waugh and Mark Taylor during the more or less unbroken run of success enjoyed by Australia in both Test and one-day cricket between 1995 and 2008, the ultimate test for Ponting came against India, especially away from home. His popularity had waned because of the bombastic approach of his players in a series in Australia the previous season when India were unlucky to lose 1-2, but there were more serious signs of relative decay in both his own batting and the team's performances when they lost 0-2 in India in 2008-09.

The team's defeats in India during his time had much to do with his own repeated disappointments there. He failed to play a single substantial Test innings in India but had his revenge on his home pitches, making 242 in defeat at Adelaide in 2003-04 followed by 257 at Sydney in the next Test to ensure victory and a share of the series. He averages 47 against India overall. He had scored more than 20,000 runs for Australia in Tests and one-day matches, despite his loss of form in 2008-09, a relative failure that contributed to the home series defeat by South Africa that threatened the end of Australia's command of world cricket. But he led a team with several fresh players to immediate revenge in South Africa. At that stage only Don Bradman and his teammate Michael Hussey had higher Test averages.

46. KEN BARRINGTON

Kenneth Frank Barrington, born 24 November 1930, Reading, UK; d. 14 March 1981, Bridgetown, Barbados

First-class: 31,714 runs (45.63), 273 wickets (32.61) and 511 catches
Tests (82): 6,806 runs (58.67), 29 wickets (44.82) and 58 catches

Craggy-jawed, crinkly-haired, beaky-nosed, brawny-armed, dark-eyed and defiant, Ken Barrington was frequently England's rock whenever they were in trouble during a life devoted to cricket. He was a batsman of high class who cut the frills that were still part of his batting when he first got into the Test side in 1955, halfway through Surrey's long period of supremacy in the County Championship, to become the epitome of the bulldog spirit.

Series against Australia inspired him most – he averaged 63.94 against them in 39 Test innings – but whenever he pulled on his cap

to go out to bat for England he gave 100 per cent concentration to the cause. Often this meant the application of a rigid defence, to the extent that he was once, rather absurdly, dropped for slow scoring after a match that England had won easily against New Zealand in 1965. At heart, however, he was an entertainer with a penchant for mimicry, dressing-room repartee and, less consciously, the occasional muddled metaphor. He would talk of batsmen 'hanging on by their eyelashes', the ball falling into 'any man's land' or of someone 'playing a great innings in anyone's cup of tea'.

When the cricket was not too serious he would fool about in the field too, to the amusement of crowds, especially Indian ones. He reached exactly a fifth of his twenty Test centuries with a six, as if to say that if only his country's reputation had not been at stake he could have played like that all the time.

He did, in fact, have all the strokes at his command, not least, being broad and stocky, the pull and square-cut. He was also a powerful driver, with the full blade of a broad-looking Stuart Surridge bat. The covers were regularly pierced even when he switched from an orthodox to an open-chested stance, the better, he felt, to deal with the short-pitched bowling that he attracted, especially from the West Indian pair Wes Hall and Charlie Griffith. He was a fine fielder anywhere, and a genuine leg-spin and googly bowler who would have been very effective in that role had he been brought up on harder wickets abroad. He took seven for 40 for MCC against Griqualand West at Kimberley on the 1964-65 tour of South Africa

Consistency and reliability were his middle names. He scored 63, 132 not out, 101 and 94 in the last four Test innings of his first trip to Australia in 1961-62 and a total of 1,763 first-class runs on the tour at an average of 80. That was the second of three successive winter tours in which he scored more than 1,000 runs, averaging 69 in India and Pakistan and 86 in South Africa. In England he scored 1,000 runs in twelve seasons and over 2,000 in three. His highest Test score was the 256 in eleven hours and 25 minutes with which, helped by Ted Dexter, he saved the Old Trafford Test of 1964.

In his all-too-brief retirement he managed a garage in Surrey and became the wise and popular manager/coach of England on overseas tours. A mild heart attack, suffered in Australia in 1968, had ended his career, and a fatal one followed in the West Indies in 1981 when he was stressed by political troubles and a struggling team. He was widely mourned.

45. CLYDE WALCOTT

Sir Clyde Leopold Walcott, b. 17 January 1926, Bridgetown, Barbados; d. 26 August 2006, Bridgetown

First-class: 11,820 runs (56.55), 35 wickets (36.25), 175 catches and 33 stumpings
Tests (44): 3,798 runs (56.68), eleven wickets (37.09), 53 catches and eleven stumpings

The tallest and hardest-hitting of the immortal 'three Ws' – Walcott, Weekes and Worrell – Clyde Walcott was both a brutal and a scintillating batsman. His confidence and physical power made him an integral part of the great forward surge enjoyed by the West Indies teams after the Second World War, and by dominating good bowling as he often did he blazed a trail for other commanding players such as Clive Lloyd, Vivian Richards and Chris Gayle. Walcott's special glories were full-blooded square-cuts and cover drives.

He was only sixteen and still at Harrison College in Bridgetown when he first played for Barbados, only twenty when he and Frank Worrell compiled the record fourth-wicket stand for Barbados against Trinidad. Walcott's score was 314 not out. Yet, despite his height, six foot two, and his broad-shouldered bulk, it was as a wicket-keeper that he first made the Test side. When he handed on the gloves he became instead a brilliant slip catcher.

His first big impact as a batsman came in India between 1948 and 1950. He scored 452 runs in five Tests at 64 and five centuries on the

tour. He improved that to seven centuries in England in 1950, powering his way to 1,674 runs, including the pounding 168 not out in the Lord's Test that paved the way for a victory that was subsequently made famous in a calypso. England's first two wickets in that game were: Hutton stumped Walcott bowled Valentine 35; Washbrook stumped Walcott bowled Ramadhin 36. These were the highest individual scores in the innings. The tide had turned.

The really purple patch in Walcott's career came, however, soon after. Within 27 months between 1953 and 1955 Walcott hammered the respective attacks of India, England and Australia for ten hundreds in twelve successive Tests. England were on the receiving end of his 228 at Bridgetown but it was the following season, 1954-55, that his peak achievement came: 827 runs in three Tests against Australia including a century in each innings at both Port of Spain and Kingston. Australia won the series but Lindwall, Miller, Benaud and Bill Johnston were among those put to the sword.

Like Worrell and Everton Weekes, Walcott wore his fame lightly off the field. He had a smile as big as his frame and a calm, very deep voice with the distinctive Bajan lilt that put the emphasis in his name on the 'cott'. He managed several West Indies sides in the 1970s, served on the cricket boards of Barbados and the West Indies for many years, and was president of the WICB, and then of the ICC at a time when his style of quiet diplomacy was needed to steer a path between the differing viewpoints of England and Australia on one side and an increasingly ambitious India, supported by the other Asian countries, on the other. He was awarded an OBE and then a knighthood for his services to the game.

44. GRAHAM GOOCH

Graham Alan Gooch, b. 23 July 1953, Leytonstone, Essex

First-class: 44,841 runs (49.11), 246 wickets (34.37) and 555 catches
Tests (118): 8,900 runs (42.58), 23 wickets (46.47) and 103 catches

One-day internationals: (125): 4,290 runs (36.98) 36 wickets (42.11) and 45 catches

Cricket's greatest players have come in all shapes and sizes. Graham Gooch emerged from the London end of Essex as a tall, heavy-footed, shambling-gaited, rosy-faced lad some way removed from the 'beau' ideal of athleticism; but you had only to see him little more than flick two sixes into the Lord's Grandstand in 1975, one of them off Jeff Thomson, a few months after the same irrepressible 'Thommo' had proved too fast and furious for England in Australia, to know that a special talent had emerged.

It took time to do so. Gooch suffered a pair in his first Test at Edgbaston that season in bowler-friendly conditions and it was not until his 21st Test against Australia that he finally got some serious revenge, with 196 at the Oval in 1985; but his natural talent against fast bowling remained. Opening the batting suited him. Tall, broad and developing a stance that told quick bowlers he was ready for them, with his bat cocked at shoulder height as they approached and his head turned over his left shoulder to keep his eyes level, he became the best player of blinding speed in the world, punishing any-thing wayward in length or direction with crisp strokes of a heavy bat. This was at a time when some of the fastest bowlers ever seen had been given licence, partly by the wearing of helmets, to bowl almost as many bouncers as they liked.

By unusual diligence, an intelligence not always evident from his 'estuary' English, and an unyielding determination to make the most of himself by keeping himself fit with long early-morning runs that remained his virtuous habit into middle age, he became England's most professional batsman in a long career devoted to the game. Not unlike his best English contemporary, David Gower, he was more vulnerable to gentler swing bowling than extreme pace, but unlike his teammate and occasional rival, Gooch could apply himself to run-scoring in any match of any duration. He was the pillar round which Essex built years of unprecedented success.

His mountain of runs, in Test and one-day cricket, was eventually higher than any man before him had built. Since the war only Graeme Hick, who did not have the same stomach for the

international circuit, has exceeded his 128 centuries. Against the almost invincible West Indies in 1980 and the following winter he scored Test centuries at Lord's, Bridgetown and Sabina Park, but his greatest Test innings – as assessed by a computer which took into account all circumstances – was his 154 not out in gloomy weather on a tricky pitch at Headingley against Ambrose, Patrick Patterson, Walsh and Marshall in 1991. It contributed 61 per cent of England's total of 252. Viv Richards with 73, Richie Richardson with 68 and Robin Smith with 54 made the only other fifties in a low-scoring game. England won by 115 runs. By all criteria, whatever a computer may say, it was one of the noblest innings ever played.

Gooch disqualified himself from England for three years by leading a 'rebel' side in South Africa, where he made what then seemed like big money and, as usual, scored heavily. It did not prevent his being made captain of England at the end of 1989, inspiring a late profusion of international runs that peaked at Lord's in 1993 when his 333 and 123 in benign conditions at Lord's against India outdid Bradman and everyone else for the highest individual aggregate in a Test match.

He was a useful medium-paced bowler and fine slip catcher throughout his career. He has remained closely involved in cricket, coaching Essex and also England on a tour of Australia but, as much as he enjoys his evenings and the best red wine, he misses the challenge of going out to bat.

43. HERBERT SUTCLIFFE

Herbert Sutcliffe, b. 24 November 1894, Harrogate; d. 22 January 1978, Cross Hills, Yorkshire

First-class: 50,670 runs (52.02), ten wickets (52.70) and 474 catches
Tests (54): 4,555 runs (60.73) and 23 catches

Post-war Yorkshire folk wanting someone to bat in defence of their life would choose either Leonard Hutton or Geoffrey Boycott. Those of earlier generations would settle without hesitation for Herbert Sutcliffe, England's rock between the wars and the other half of famous opening partnerships for England with Jack Hobbs and for Yorkshire with Percy Holmes.

There has never been a more consistent batsman. Serenity was his greatest quality: according to R.C. Robertson-Glasgow, he was the sort of man who would 'rather miss a train than be seen in disorder and breathing heavily'. He played countless long innings yet, batting without a cap unless the sun was especially hot, photographs suggest that there was never a moment even in any of his many long innings when a single strand of his neatly groomed hair fell out of place.

Lean, fit and muscular, he showed bottomless courage and unlimited concentration, and when the bowling was exceptionally fast or the pitch especially awkward he could be relied upon to excel. There was none of Hobbs' grace or obvious pedigree about his batting, which was functional and simple. He kept the face of his bat open, quickly assessed length, and played with the full face of the bat before breaking the wrists to keep the ball down when defending. Anything short would be cut, pulled or hooked. He was a superb judge of a run, always prepared to go for the quick single.

Of his extraordinary number of 145 opening partnerships of 100 or more, 74 were with Holmes and 26 with Hobbs, with whom he shared comfortably the most reliable pairing ever seen. Their average partnership was 87. The alliance started in 1924 against South Africa, with stands of 136 and 268. Sutcliffe himself, all the better for starting Test cricket as a mature player, never looked back from his hundred at Lord's in his second Test.

His wonderful record against Australia started with a glorious tour in 1924-25 when he and Hobbs put on 157, 110 and 283 in England's first three innings of the series. Sutcliffe averaged 81 for his 734 runs in the series, and reached 1,000 Test runs in only twelve innings. Australia won that series, but the Ashes were regained by England at home in 1926 when Sutcliffe's 161 in the second innings made possible the decisive victory at the Oval. He averaged better than 50 in each of the four more series that he played against Australia, and

66.85 in 27 matches against them overall.

The immaculate Herbert scored more than 2,000 runs each season between 1922 and 1935 and in 1932, a wet summer, he somehow managed fourteen centuries and 3,336 runs. His opening partnership of 555 with Holmes against Essex at Leyton that season was the first-class record for 45 years.

Sutcliffe's arrival for Yorkshire had been delayed by the First World War and his career was curtailed by the second. He served in both, rising to the rank of Major before becoming a successful businessman. It was just reward for a man whose life was disciplined from dawn until dark. His son Billy, christened William Herbert Hobbs, went on to captain Yorkshire.

42. P.B.H. MAY

Peter Barker Howard May, b. 31 December 1929, Reading; d. 27 December 1994, Liphook, Hampshire

First-class: 27,592 runs (51.00) and 282 catches
Tests (66): 4,537 runs (46.77) and 42 catches

The precision of Peter May's batting was like one of those sunny winter mornings when a sharp frost has frozen away all muddiness, leaving trees and buildings etched in clean lines against the blueness of the sky.

Bare-headed except when hot weather demanded a cap, his hair was short and always immaculate above sharp features and broad shoulders. His kit, too, was always pristine white. A carefully cared-for Stuart Surridge bat moved in straight lines through the path of the ball, sending it skimming past mid-off or mid-on, not with a Pietersen whip of the wrists but with the full face extended until the ball hit the

boundary. He was the most professional of all amateurs, although firmness of purpose was never confused with anything underhand or unsporting.

Like his predecessor as England captain, Len Hutton, the man known respectfully by every colleague and opponent as 'P.B.H' was uncomfortable with the public esteem and attention that his eminence attracted. He never lacked inner steel or confidence but he was shy, perhaps from being a prodigy adulated even in his schooldays at Charterhouse, always courteous and modest to a fault. He could enjoy team camaraderie as much as anyone, but he was happier with his wife and four daughters at home than he was in a bar talking cricket.

Against an unclear background he never saw the first ball bowled to him in a Test match, against South Africa at Leeds, but he pushed out in hope and went on to make 100 at the age of 21. He had not yet had his third year at Cambridge, but quite soon he was the best batsman in England.

The responsibilities that entailed, together with the captaincy and the close attentions of a press that he would rather have kept at a greater distance, shortened his career. He still made more than 1,000 runs in fourteen seasons and above 2,000 in five of them. He captained Surrey from 1957 to 1962, and England 41 times.

His 285 at Edgbaston in 1957, when his partnership with Colin Cowdrey added 411 for the fourth wicket, drew the sting from Sonny Ramadhin's mysterious spin. He averaged 97.80 in the series. In 21 Tests against Australia he scored 1,566 runs at 46, sharing in the home triumphs of 1953 and 1956 when he had the pleasure of leading one of the strongest bowling sides England have ever had.

The short-lived period of English supremacy was abruptly ended in Australia in 1958-59; yet he played one of his most majestic innings on that tour, against an Australian XI at Sydney, scoring his second hundred of the match between lunch and tea on the third day.

Illness in the West Indies in 1959-60 forced him home early and he played only four more Tests, at home to Australia in 1961, before retiring to an insurance job in the City. His strong sense of duty to cricket remained, however. Both locally and nationally he took on several roles as president and chairman, and he was chairman of England's selectors from 1982 to 1988.

41. RICHIE BENAUD

Richard Benaud, b. 6 October 1930, Penrith, New South Wales

First-class: 11,719 runs (36.50), 945 wickets (24.73) and 254 catches
Tests (63): 2,201 runs (24.45), 248 wickets (27.03) and 65 catches

Few cricketers have been so famous for so long as Richie Benaud, a household name first as an all-round cricketer of style and flair in all departments, then as the smoothest and fairest of television commentators. His distinctive voice has been imitated more than that of any commentator save John Arlott's, and few former Test players have been so generous about the abilities and attitudes of the next generation of players.

Apart from his talent as a classical leg-spin bowler, hard-hitting batsman and brilliant fielder, Benaud, from Huguenot stock (he bought a house in the French village that bears his name), was probably the best captain Australia has ever had. He was outstanding in every aspect of the job: quick to read a game at every stage and to seize opportunities to get on top; decisive and respected in the dressing-room yet popular too; a skilful, witty interpreter of events to the media; and hard but scrupulously fair. (The fact that, in 1958-59, he led bowlers like Ian Meckiff, Gordon Rorke and Keith Slater, all of whom had highly suspect actions, was not his fault.)

Lou Benaud, his father, was a first-grade player who once took twenty wickets in a match, and his younger brother John also played for New South Wales as well as averaging 44 in three Tests for Australia.

Richie first played for his state at eighteen and for Australia at 21, against the West Indies in 1951-2. He hit eleven sixes in an innings in the 1953 Scarborough Festival after his first Ashes series, but it was as a leg-spin bowler of great accuracy and carefully practised variations that he became his country's leading wicket-taker. He had a brilliant all-round tour of the Caribbean in 1957-58, hitting four centuries and taking 106 wickets.

Having organised the dismantling of England's formidable team at home in 1958-59 – for all the talk of 'chuckers', his own pure bowling took 31 wickets in five Tests at only eighteen runs each – he led by example again in Pakistan and India in 1959-60, taking 47 Test wickets at 20.19.

At home to the West Indies in 1960-61 he and Frank Worrell seemed determined to have an entertaining series and, following the Brisbane tie, the cricket captured the public imagination to such an extent that the crowd at Melbourne on the second day of the fifth Test in February totalled 90,800, officially a record attendance for a day's cricket.

As a bowler, Benaud's six for 70 at Old Trafford in the decisive Test of the 1961 series was probably his finest hour. Chasing 256 to win in the fourth innings, England were 150 for one before Benaud went round the wicket to exploit the rough and took five for twelve in 25 balls.

Thorough and meticulous in everything he has done in life, he had prepared for his role in the media by working part-time in various areas of journalism before he retired from playing. In a pithy style, he has written regular columns for the Murdoch press in Australia and England for more than 40 years but it is as a succinct and shrewd commentator, especially for the Channel Nine network in Australia and the BBC, that many will remember him. In 2009 he said that he would retire after one more season, at the age of 79.

40. FRANK WOOLLEY

Frank Edward Woolley, b. 27 May 1887, Tonbridge; d. 18 October 1978, Halifax, Novia Scotia

First-class: 58,959 runs (40.77), 2,066 wickets (19.77) and 1,018 catches
Tests (64): 3,283 runs (36.07), 83 wickets (33.91) and 64 catches

Some great players were revered for their consistency, some for their ability to entertain, some because a special aesthetic beauty so pleased the eye. Frank Woolley of Kent and England managed all three.

He was a left-handed batsman; a slow left-arm bowler with a curving run whose left hand was hidden behind his back until the delivery, like Colin Blythe's; and a voracious slip catcher, especially off Tich Freeman's leg-breaks. When all his first-class figures have been marvelled at once more, what remains is the impression of unrivalled grace left behind by his batting.

H.S. Altham recalled his tall, graceful figure and the majestic, almost casual command of his stroke play. R.C. Robertson-Glasgow remembered from personal experience how his long reach, and the power of his pendulum swing, could muddle a bowler's length. 'Balls that you felt had a right to tax him he would hit airily over your head.' There was, he added poignantly in a piece written during the Second World War, 'all summer in a stroke by Woolley.'

E.W. Swanton explained the pure simplicity of the batting method that earned him his monumental stockpile of 58,959 runs, second only to Hobbs:

Here was this extremely tall slim figure, swinging his bat in the fullest and truest pendulum through the line of the ball. There were no kinks or ornamentations ... Here comes the ball, there goes the foot, down she comes and through.

Yet this straightest of drivers off either foot was also a delicate late cutter and, like David Gower, his nearest replica since, a pretty deflector to fine-leg of the ball rising to his hip.

If Woolley had a fault as a cricketer, it was unwariness. He batted the same way, it seemed, whatever the situation and whoever was bowling, with an air of casual indifference. Utterly unselfish, he would take on a bowler with whom his partner at the time was obviously struggling unequally. 'The thing he never seemed to contemplate, let alone to fear,' wrote Swanton, 'was getting out himself. He was the antithesis of the calculating, bread-and-butter run collector.'

To an extent perhaps that explains why only five of his 145 first-class centuries were scored in his 64 Test matches. Two of his most remarkable innings, after all, were the 95 and 93 that he made in thrilling resistance to the otherwise invincible Gregory and McDonald at Lord's in 1921.

His hundred at Sydney in 1924-25 was scored in two and a half hours. Such triumphs for England were disappointingly few, yet he scored more than 1,000 runs in 28 seasons and took 100 wickets in eight of them. Even Woolley could, as the professionals say, fill his boots. He scored 305 not out for MCC against Tasmania on the tour of 1911-12, and in 1928 twelve hundreds took his season's tally to 3,352.

A reserved and sober man with a gentle sense of humour, he remained straight-backed into his nineties. He married a Canadian lady late in life.

39. FRANK WORRELL

Sir Frank Mortimore Maglinne Worrell, b. 1 August 1924, Bridgetown, Barbados; d. 13 March 1967, Kingston, Jamaica

First-class: 15,025 runs (54.24), 349 wickets (28.98) and 139 catches
Tests (51): 3,860 runs (49.48), 69 wickets (38.73) and 43 catches

'Whom the Gods love die young,' and Sir Frank Worrell died at the age of only 42. The worldwide esteem in which he was held was reflected in a memorial service held in Westminster Abbey shortly after his death.

Revered as a cricketer of grace and style, a man of moral strength and dignity who ended forever any suggestion that a black man might not be worthy to lead the countries of the West Indies in unity, he was both a great all-rounder and a great leader.

Like Gary Sobers after him, Worrell started his cricketing life primarily as a slow left-arm bowler. He was a prodigy at Combermere

School but became a brisk new-ball swing bowler too. Slim and stylish, his batting had an unhurried ease but it was only when he took his chance as a night watchman to make 64 not out that his potential was realised. Up the order, he made 188 and 68 in the next match against Trinidad.

At 19 he scored 308 not out for Barbados, sharing an unbroken stand of 502 with John Goddard against Trinidad at Bridgetown. Two years later, in 1945-46, poor Trinidad suffered again when Worrell and Clyde Walcott made 574 together for the same fourth wicket, this time at Port of Spain. He scored 97 in his first Test, against England in 1947-48, and 131 not out at Georgetown.

By now he was playing for Jamaica and in 1948 he signed for Radcliffe in the Lancashire League, taking 66 wickets and averaging 88 with the bat. Touring India with a Commonwealth side the following winter, he scored more than 1,600 runs with five centuries and averaged 74 in the unofficial Tests. His prolific form continued on the famous tour of England in 1950 when Worrell, with 539 runs in the series, including 261 at Trent Bridge and 138 at the Oval, was the leading batsman.

Against Australia in 1951-52 he was again the heaviest scorer and took six for 38 at Adelaide to bowl them out for 88. Then, in India in 1951-52, the 'three Ws' legend reached its zenith, with Worrell scoring 237 in the fifth match at Sabina Park and sharing stands of 197 with Weekes and 213 with Walcott.

Returning to England in 1957 he ended a lean spell with a productive tour that included a cultured innings of 191 not out at Trent Bridge, where he carried his bat and then took seven for 70 in England's only innings at Headingley. He gave England further trouble at Bridgetown in the next series at home, 1959-60, scoring 197 not out in the first Test at Bridgetown, where he batted for eleven and a half hours. But his imperishable fame rests on his captaincy of two tours that captured public imagination in an extraordinary way.

In Australia he and Richie Benaud opposed each other in the series that began with the Brisbane tied Test in December 1960 and ended with a tickertape parade in Melbourne for the departing touring team. In England in 1963 it was the Lord's Test match that finished in unbearable tension. All four results were possible when the final ball arrived. Worrell, as he had been at Brisbane, was the calmest man on the field. 'Don't bowl a no ball,' he said to Wes Hall.

Worrell had read sociology at Manchester University and before being struck down by leukaemia he had embarked on a career at the University of the West Indies in Bridgetown, where the beautiful modern cricket ground at Cave Hill is named after the 'three Ws'. He had been knighted by the Queen three years before his death, and as a man of strong convictions and exemplary character he would surely have become a statesman of high renown if he had lived.

38. GREG CHAPPELL

Gregory Stephen Chappell, b. 7 August 1948, Adelaide

First-class: 24,535 runs (52.20), 291 wickets (29.95) and 376 catches
Tests (87): 7,110 runs (53.86), 47 wickets (40 .70) and 122 catches
One-day internationals (74): 2,331 runs (40.18), 72 wickets (29.12) and 23 catches

At the age of 22 in 1970-71, Greg Chappell made a century in his first Test at the WACA ground in Perth with the air of someone doing only what was expected of him. He had come to the wicket at 107 for five after England had scored 397. His batting always had a look of lofty authority, perfect poise and utter composure.

Despite distractions, responsibilities and imperfect health, he finished with a Test average of 53 that was altogether worthy of his exalted quality. Excluding those still playing, it is Australia's highest excepting only Bradman, and it would have been even better had his prolific series in 1971-72, when a Rest of the World side stood in for the banned South Africans, been taken into account.

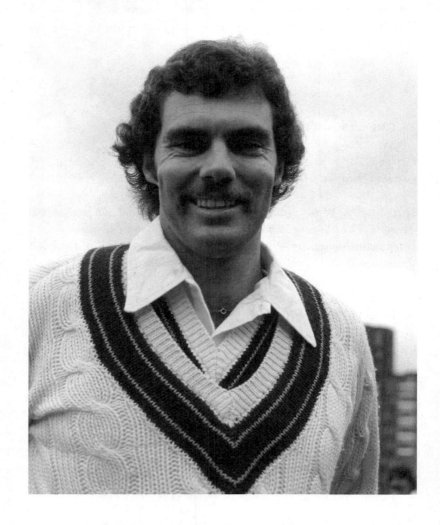

He was one of three maternal grandsons of the former Australian captain Victor Richardson, all of whom played Test cricket. His elder brother, Ian, was a player of very high calibre himself, a forceful character who led a mighty side in the 1970s. Greg, inscrutable and more inclined to keep his own counsel, became a part of his sibling's team and, in time, the best Australian batsman of a momentous era. He succeeded Ian as Test captain in 1976-77, when the game was about to change forever as a consequence of Kerry Packer's challenge to the established order.

Tall, slim and never unbalanced, he was quick to decide whether to defend with the straightest of blades or to attack with a complete variety of strokes – majestic drives on either side of the wicket, crisp and fearless hooks or precise cuts and leg glances. He was a quite brilliant fielder at second slip and a useful bowler of medium-paced inswingers.

Starting with South Australia but playing later for Queensland, he broadened his education by playing for Somerset in 1968. On his first tour of England in 1972 he made immaculate hundreds in the Lord's and Oval Test matches. At the Oval Ian made one too – a unique fraternal double which they bettered in New Zealand in 1973-74 when, at the Basin Reserve pitch in Wellington, Ian scored 145 and 121, and Greg 247 not out and 133.

It was his arrival in his brother's side that turned it into the best in the world. He scored 608 runs at 55 as the Ashes were regained in 1974-75 and in his first match as captain, against the West Indies at Brisbane, made a hundred in each innings, which constituted another record.

The pressure was stepped up for all international cricketers after the disbandment of World Series Cricket because of the proliferation of one-day internationals. Chappell's relatively frail physique felt the strain at times but he remained a brilliant batsman in all forms of the game, despite having to wait until 1982-83 to achieve his ambition of leading Australia in a winning Ashes series.

His reputation took a high-profile battering when he ordered his brother Trevor to bowl an underarm grubber when the last ball of an international arrived with New Zealand needing six to win, but that was symptomatic of the more ruthless and materialistic approach that

WSC had encouraged. He finished in glory with an innings of 182 in his last Test against Pakistan to pass Bradman's record Test aggregate.

While others like Border and Steve Waugh showed even more stamina in the new order of non-stop cricket, Greg was content to play his part as a coach. The fitness levels and fielding routines that he introduced during his two years in charge of the India team helped to make them a more successful team away from home.

37. GRAEME POLLOCK

Robert Graeme Pollock, b. 27 February 1944, Durban

First-class: 20,940 runs (54.67), 43 wickets (47.95) and 248 catches
Tests (23): 2,256 runs (60.97), four wickets (51.00) and seventeen catches

Graeme Pollock walked at the age of eight months, played for Grey High School in Port Elizabeth aged thirteen, scored a century in the highly competitive Currie Cup at sixteen and made 1,000 runs on a tour of Australia before he was twenty. By then he was a strapping six foot three inch left-hander who hit the ball with tremendous force by the straight and simple swing of a heavy bat. He was capable, too, of strokes of delicate finesse. He had a wide stance that allowed him to shift his weight either way and without hurry into the path of the ball.

Seven centuries in 23 Tests and an average of 60 left everyone wanting more but just when he, his fast-bowling brother Peter, Barry Richards, Colin Bland and Mike Procter had emerged as the pillars of South Africa's best-ever white cricket team, they were dis-qualified from official international cricket because of South Africa's apartheid system.

His father, a Scot by birth, kept wicket for the Orange Free State.

News of the boy's genius reached England early because his school coach was the gregarious George Cox of Sussex fame. In his second first-class match against a combined Australia XI in Perth he scored a century in 88 minutes. A maiden Test century followed at Sydney, and in Adelaide he played an exhilarating innings of 175.

He became the youngest player to pass 1,000 Test runs during the course of an innings in the 1965 Test at Trent Bridge that will never be forgotten by any who saw it. Coming in at sixteen for two, and soon seeing South Africa slip further to 43 for four, he played on his own exalted plane for 125 in two hours and twenty minutes, while 35 runs were scored from the other end. He stroked 21 fours, mainly through the off side. In 70 minutes after lunch, before being caught at slip off Tom Cartwright, he scored 90 out of 102. With his brother taking ten for 87, South Africa went on to beat England for the first time for ten years and to win the series.

He did something similar to Australia at Cape Town in 1966-67, coming in at twelve for two and soon seeing the innings subside further to 85 for five. Despite a strained thigh that confined him mainly to shots off the back foot, he scored 100 off 139 balls and went on to make 209. A week earlier his run-a-minute 90 had helped South Africa to their first home victory against Australia, and another century followed at Port Elizabeth.

There was a last hurrah in 1969-70 when he scored 272 at Durban in the 4-0 humiliation of Australia but the rest of his career was destined to be appreciated only by a few, including an innings of 222 in a 60-over Gillette Cup match in Port Elizabeth and record aggregates in the Currie Cup for both Eastern Province and the Transvaal. He was able to play in a Rest of the World team in England and in unofficial Tests against 'rebel' West Indian sides in 1983 and 1984. Centuries in two of the unofficial Tests showed him, even when well past his prime, to be capable still of humbling the fiercest fast bowling.

36. WAQAR YOUNIS

Waqar Younis Maitla, b. 16 November 1971, Vihari, Punjab

First-class: 2,972 runs (13.38), 956 wickets (22.53) and 58 catches
Tests (87): 1,010 runs, 373 wickets (23.56) and eighteen catches
One-day internationals (262): 969 runs (10.30), 416 wickets (23.84) and
35 catches

A chance sight of Waqar Younis bowling on television in 1989 in a match between the one-day champions of India and Pakistan persuaded the Pakistan captain, Imran Khan, to go straight to the ground in Lahore to have a look at the young fast bowler in the flesh. He was sufficiently impressed to take him with the national team to a training camp in Sharjah, and it was quickly evident that a champion had arrived.

Forever associated with Wasim Akram, his new-ball bowling partner for Pakistan, Waqar was a surging force of nature, one of the most thrilling and wholehearted fast bowlers there has ever been. A sturdy six-footer, he hurled himself towards the batsman after a longish run-up that left no one in doubt about the threat he posed. His wickets in Test cricket were taken at an extraordinary strike rate of 43 balls per wicket, eleven balls a wicket better than Wasim, and no fewer than 57 per cent of his victims were either bowled (27 per cent) or leg before wicket. By comparison, another equally successful modern bowler, Dennis Lillee, who bowled more often on bouncier pitches in Australia, had 67 per cent of his victims caught, only 32 per cent bowled or LBW.

Waqar could bowl as fierce a bouncer as anyone, but on the slow, dry pitches of the subcontinent his intention was to pitch the ball up and to make it swing, at great pace. He made a new ball leave the right-hander and an old one swing in viciously late towards the batsman's toes. Only Joel Garner had a more feared yorker than Waqar's

- 48 per cent of Garner's 259 Test wickets were bowled or leg before, but his six foot eight inches of height allowed him exceptional bounce: 51 per cent of his victims were caught.

As Imran Khan never ceased to point out, Pakistani cricket had no proper pyramid structure that allowed the best cricketers a path from school to the Test side, and Waqar took an unconventional route to the top. Born in the Vihari district of the Punjab (his official birth date has been questioned), Waqar's father was the eldest of five children of a cotton farmer, who took a job in Sharjah when Waqar was three. Waqar had four years at Sharjah College, where he was inspired by the sight of Imran bowling in a tournament, then moved to Sadiq Public School in Bahawalpur, where his athletic talent was nurtured. He started his first-class career in Multan, got a contract with United Bank and was picked for the Pakistan under-nineteen side before Imran gave his career the final push.

After ten Tests he had already taken 50 wickets, 29 of them in a three-match series against New Zealand at home in 1990-91. His 22 wickets in England in 1992 helped to win Pakistan the series, although the team's success was tarnished by allegations of ball-tampering – using artificial means to rough up one side in order to help the ball to swing in the opposite direction to the shine. It did not visibly unsettle Waqar, who took nine for 81 in an innings against New Zealand at Hamilton in 1992-93 and nineteen in three Tests in the West Indies, followed by a more easily acquired 27 in three games at home to Zimbabwe. He reached 150 wickets in his 27th Test and his bowling in one-day internationals was no less devastating. His 416 wickets in these 50-over matches were taken on average every 30 balls.

As much a rival as a partner to Wasim he later faded in and out of the Pakistan side, the result of both back trouble and the mysterious internal politics that sometimes make his country's selection decisions unfathomable. He played for Surrey from 1990 to 1993, in 1991 taking 113 wickets at only fourteen runs each, and in 1997 he returned to county cricket to help Glamorgan win the Championship. Warwickshire engaged him for one-day games in 2003.

35. K.S. RANJITSINHJI

Kumar Shri Ranjitsinhji, b. 10 September 1872, Sarodar, Kathiawar; d. 2 April 1933, Jamnagar Palace, Gujarat

First-class: 24,692 runs (56.37), 133 wickets (34.59) and 234 catches
Tests (15): 989 runs (44.95), one wicket (39) and thirteen catches

The fabled Ranji was an original, the most brilliant batsman of his time, a champion of back-foot play and the inventor of the leg glance, by which he took the wind from the sails of the fastest bowlers with a quick step across his stumps and an impudent flick of the wrists, to send straight balls skimming like pucks to the fine-leg boundary.

This was pure genius and the cricketer of minor princely blood, born in poverty in rural India, became a popular hero, the first famous international sportsman with a dark skin. It is some indication of the esteem in which he was held, by both the public and the leading amateurs of the day, that he was invited to play not just for England but, including one-off festival games, for seventeen different first-class teams.

He had learned only the basics of the game at an exclusive school in India where his fees were paid by the Jam Sahib of Nawanagar, a distant relative who had briefly considered adopting the boy. So unorthodox were his methods as he began to take the game more seriously that it took him four seasons at Cambridge before he was given a game for the University eleven. It has been accepted, if never proved, that he had already scored three hundreds in three separate club matches in Cambridge on the same day. Coached by Dan Hayward of the famous Cambridgeshire cricketing family, Ranji won Blues in 1893 (under F.S. Jackson) and 1894.

He went to Brighton to begin his scintillating career for Sussex in 1895, forming county cricket's most prolific partnership with C.B. Fry, who famously said that Ranji could have played three different strokes to every ball he received. In his fist match for Sussex he scored

77 and 150 not out against MCC at Lord's, and by the end of the season had made 1,775 runs, vying for the headlines with W.G. Grace.

Test cricket followed in 1896, when he broke one of Grace's records by scoring 2,781 runs in the season, with ten centuries. At Old Trafford in his first Test he scored 62 and 154 out of 305 against Australia. George Giffen wrote soon after: 'Ranji is the batting wonder of the age. His play was a revelation to us, with his marvellous cutting and extraordinary hitting to leg.' He averaged twice as many in this first series as any other batsman on either side.

In 1897 he came close to reaching 2,000 runs again, then at Sydney in the first Test of the 1897-98 series made a glorious 175, despite feeling unwell. In 1899 he saved England from defeat at Trent Bridge and he became the first batsman to score 3,000 runs in a season, a feat he repeated the following year when he made five double centuries. He scored at least 1,000 runs in every season in which he was able to play regularly, and 72 centuries from his 307 games overall.

Popularity did not equate to wealth. In 1902, not yet having succeeded to the title of Maharajah, Ranji's financial problems brought him close to bankruptcy. Having returned to India he made a successful claim for the vacant princely throne of his patron, a decision made in 1907 by British colonial civil servants who were undoubtedly swayed by his fame on the cricket field. It transformed his wealth and social standing and he was able to play more cricket in England, although no longer in Tests, from 1908. Later he served with Fry on the League of Nations, lost an eye in a shooting accident and divided his time between ruling his state and living the life of an aristocrat in England.

34. WASIM AKRAM

Wasim Akram, b. 3 June 1966, Lahore

First-class: 7,161 runs (22.63), 1,042 wickets (21.64) and 97 catches
Tests (104): 2,898 runs (22.64), 414 wickets (23.62) and 44 catches

One-day internationals (356): 3,717 runs (16.52), 502 wickets (23.52) and 88 catches

I shall not forget my first sight of Wasim Akram, a thin slip of a lad cutting through the wind at the Melbourne Cricket Ground with a brisk, eager approach and a whippy action to take the first five Australian wickets for thirteen in a one-day international at Melbourne. Already he had taken seven for 50 on his first-class debut in Pakistan at the age of eighteen, and twelve wickets in his first two Tests in New Zealand in 1984-85.

Only Gary Sobers and Alan Davidson can compare with Wasim as the finest left-handed all-rounder. Not in Sobers' class as a batsman but capable of the occasional volcanic innings, he was a more lethal swing bowler, always dangerous with a new ball and often irresistible with an old one. He was, too, a charismatic cricketer who not only inspired teammates but excited spectators. The game could never be dull when Wasim was involved.

Tall and slim, although he broadened his physique in his maturity, he ran to the stumps at great speed with short strides and always had excellent control of in-swing and out-swing. Sometimes he would bowl a succession of bouncers when a ball was just out of its wrapper, partly to get batsmen hopping about on the back foot while the bounce was at its hardest, and partly to remove the lacquer from the surface of the leather.

In England in 1987 he took sixteen Test wickets at 29, and with Imran Khan formed the first of his two outstanding international new-ball partnerships. It was with Waqar Younis that he became associated for longer, however. With the leg-spinner Mushtaq Ahmed in support, Pakistan had the most potent and varied attack in world cricket, leading to victory in the 1992 World Cup when Wasim's eighteen wickets included three vital ones in the final against England after he had thrashed 33 from eighteen balls.

Halfway through his career he was diagnosed with diabetes. He required insulin injections daily, but uncomplainingly got on with his career. His performances were mercurial but frequently inspirational. In common with only two other players, he took two Test hat-tricks,

uniquely adding two more in one-day cricket. His Test hat-tricks were both against Sri Lanka, in consecutive Tests in 1998-99. He also took four wickets in one over against the West Indies in 1990-91.

His batting was correct and attractive, based on strong driving, but also impatient. He scored 52 and a match-saving 123 against Australia in Adelaide in 1989-90, having taken eleven wickets in the previous Test in Melbourne. At Sheikhupura against Zimbabwe in October 1996, coming in at number eight with his team in danger of embarrassment, he played easily the longest innings of his life, scoring 257 not out against Zimbabwe.

Against the strongest Test opposition of the period, the West Indies, he took 21 wickets in three home Tests at home in 1990-91. In England in 1992 he took 82 wickets at sixteen and 21 in the four Tests for which he was fit but by now, with county cricket for Lancashire and non-stop international commitments at other times, his body was feeling the strain imposed by his elastic action. He lost some of his sharpness as a bowler following two operations on his groin.

Injuries, captaincy disputes, accusations of ball-tampering and, more seriously, of a connection with the match-fixing scandal – he was disqualified from the national captaincy after a Pakistan High Court judge concluded that 'he was not above suspicion' – did not prevent his setting a new record for the number of one-day international wickets, 502. He was the first bowler to take more than 400 wickets in both Tests and one-day internationals.

33. JIM LAKER

James Charles Laker, b. 9 February 1922, Saltaire, Bradford; d. 23 April 1986, London

First-class: 7,304 runs (16.60), 1,944 wickets (18.40) and 270 catches
Tests (46): 676 runs (14.08), 193 wickets (21.24) and twelve catches

Jim Laker, the down-to-earth professional who knew his great worth but never flaunted it, was the best of all orthodox off-spinners and the man who came, one week in Manchester in 1956, closer than any cricketer in history to the perfect performance. With barely a change of expression and many a hitch of his flannels he wheeled away at Old Trafford on a dry pitch (despite many interruptions for rain during the match) to take nineteen wickets, nine for 37 and ten for 53, utterly dumbfounding his opponents.

One by one on an incredible final afternoon the Australians came and went, bowled, caught in the leg-trap or plumb leg-before as they went back and the ball, delivered from round the wicket, spun sharply from outside the off stump. Tony Lock, his potent and talented spin-bowling partner for many years for both Surrey and England, took only one wicket in the match. But this was Laker's year: he had already taken all ten, for 88, against the Australians for Surrey at the Oval. In the Test series he took 46 wickets, which was a record.

When the game had been won at Old Trafford Jim took his sweater from the umpire, swung it over his left shoulder and walked off with no more than a modest smile. On the way home that night he stopped for a sandwich and a beer at a pub in Lichfield, where everyone was talking about his extraordinary feat. But no one recognised him.

Tallish and very strong, he gave the ball a tremendous rip after his sauntering run, with an audible and visible flick of strong fingers, his arm sweeping across a braced left leg. There has never been a better spin-bowling action. There was no hint of the illegal straightening of the arm that had been evident in one or two sharp spinners before him and has been in several since. He bowled long, very accurate spells on good pitches, flighting the ball and making it dip, and once there was turn, especially on a drying pitch, he was lethal.

Yorkshire born, he came to the fore in 1947 with 66 wickets for Surrey and was picked for that winter's tour of the West Indies, where he was the leading wicket-taker. Some punishment at the hands of the quick-footed Australians in 1948 meant that he was not an automatic selection for England until 1956, despite Surrey's consistent success through the 1950s. He had figures of eight for two in the Test trial at Bradford in 1950 and took 166 wickets that season, but there was an

extraordinary supply of outstanding spinners among his contemporaries, including the left-arm rivals Lock and Johnny Wardle.

Amongst off-spinners, the versatile Bob Appleyard did not play Test cricket until he was 30 because of illness, and no sooner had he seized 200 wickets for Yorkshire in 1951 than he was struck down by pleurisy. But in his first five overs in Test cricket he took four for six against Pakistan, and in 1954-55 he topped the England averages in Australia. Fred Titmus did the 100 wicket-1,000 run double eight times, made the ball curl, drift and dip like a seabird and reeled in 153 Test victims. Ray Illingworth's slight inferiority as a bowler was more than cancelled out by his batting and his captaincy.

But none of these men spun the ball as furiously as Laker. He played three seasons for Essex after falling out with Surrey and then became a popular BBC television commentator, as dry, subdued, wary and level-headed in his broadcasts as he had been on the field.

32. EVERTON WEEKES

Everton de Courcy Weekes, b. 26 February 1925, St Michael, Barbados

First-class: 12,010 runs (55.34), seventeen wickets (43.00), 125 catches and one stumping
Tests (48): 4,455 runs (58.61), one wicket (77) and 49 catches

'While Walcott bludgeoned the bowlers and Weekes dominated them, Worrell waved them away,' wrote Learie Constantine in his *Wisden* obituary of Frank Worrell, thus declaring his preference for the eldest of the three contemporary heroes of Barbados. On the island the debate about which of them was the best has raged among the cricketing cognoscenti ever since.

The verdict for most is that Everton De Courcy Weekes was, if only by a short head, the best of the three; moreover that he is, with Headley, Sobers, Richards and Lara, one of the five greatest batsmen to have played for the West Indies. Fifteen of his 36 first-class centuries were scored in his 48 Tests

He was shorter than the other 'two Ws', of stocky build, strong and quick on his feet. He hooked and cut the fast bowlers with relish and rapier force and drove hard to all directions, often giving himself room to lace the ball through the off side. He was a brilliant fielder and a shrewd captain of Barbados after deciding to withdraw from international cricket. He always had a sense of balance and life on his own beautiful island suited him very nicely, thank you.

In his prime he was a fierce and relentless batsman whose periods of form could be quite devastating. By making 141 against England in the fourth Test of 1947-48 he made certain of a place in the 1948-9 touring party to India, where he reeled off scores of 128, 194 and, in each innings at Eden Gardens, Calcutta, 162 and 101. Looking for a sixth successive Test hundred, he was run out for 90 at Madras.

He was the top scorer again on the famous tour of England in 1950 when he scored 2,310 runs at 79.65, his seven centuries including his 304 at Fenner's after the undergraduates of Cambridge had made headlines by scoring more than 500. He made four other double centuries on the tour and although the only one in a Test was his 129 at Trent Bridge, he made up for it by scoring 206 at Port of Spain in his next series against England, at home in 1953-4.

He was at his plundering best in New Zealand in 1955-56, hitting 940 runs at an average of 104 in eight first-class matches. Three of his six centuries came in the Tests. In England in 1957, however, he suffered sinus trouble and only on a tricky pitch at Lord's did his supreme class stand out. He made 90, the top score for a badly beaten team. He played one more home series before confining himself to domestic cricket and league cricket in Lancashire, where he was prolific, even as a bowler.

A cricketer who enjoyed life to the full in his youth – one future Test player with a different name was strongly rumoured to be his offspring – he was the third of the 'three Ws' to be knighted, having already been awarded first an MBE then a CBE. He coached in Barbados, commented sagely in radio broadcasts and played bridge as well as cricket for his island.

31. RAY LINDWALL

Raymond Russell Lindwall, b. 3 October 1921, Sydney; d. 23 June 1996, Brisbane

First-class: 5,042 runs (21.82), 794 wickets (21.35) and 123 catches
Tests (61): 1,502 runs (21.12), 228 wickets (23.03) and 26 catches

With his opening partner Keith Miller, Ray Lindwall was chiefly responsible for Australia's supremacy over the rest of the cricketing world in the years immediately after the Second World War. There were never any histrionics about his cricket. He was a dramatic performer not, generally, because he threatened a batsman's safety, although he was very fast indeed, but because he swung the ball lethally late and both ways.

A back foot 'dragger', he was a quite different sort of fast bowler from the 'hit the deck' type generally seen now, although there were similar features in the methods of Fred Trueman, Graham McKenzie, Waqar Younis and Darren Gough. All relied primarily on swinging the ball at pace.

Lindwall did so consistently, achieving over a longer period what Harold Larwood, another relatively small fast bowler, had in the 1930s. Lindwall himself was five foot ten inches tall, with a powerful chest and shoulders. His action had a mesmeric momentum, starting slowly but building with long, low strides, arms pumping in a manner often imitated, leading to a final stretch in which the body turned sideways and the right foot dragged through from behind the bowling crease to well beyond the 'popping' crease. It was at once dramatic and rhythmical.

There was little time for a batsman to assess whether the out-swinger or the in-swinger was humming its way towards his stumps at great velocity. A typical John Arlott commentary describes Lindwall bowling successive balls to Len Hutton in 1948. The first swings away and Hutton drives it past cover for four. The next is an in-swinger that bowls him. In 29 Tests against England alone, Lindwall took 114 wickets at 22 runs each, besides scoring 795 runs that included a storming hundred at Melbourne in 1946-47, when he and Don Tallon put on a rollicking 154 for the eighth wicket in less than an hour and a half.

Having taken eighteen wickets against India in 1947-48, including seven for 38 in the second innings at Adelaide, he enjoyed himself on and off the field in England in 1948, taking 86 wickets at fifteen on the tour. The Ashes were lost in the end in 1953 but he was nonetheless successful, taking 85 more wickets at sixteen.

Because he was less dependent on bounce than others, he was almost equally effective wherever he bowled. He took 21 Test wickets against the West Indies at home in 1951-52 and another twenty, albeit at greater cost, in the Caribbean where, at Bridgetown, he made the second of his Test hundreds. At Madras in 1956-57, his seven for 43 in the second innings won Australia a Test on the subcontinent for the first time.

Lindwall's early cricket was played in Sydney for the St George Club, for whose rugby league first-grade team he was also an outstanding full-back. He moved to Brisbane later in his career and captained Queensland from 1955 to 1960. Always popular, he had a disarming smile – which was used to great effect, no doubt, when he retired to run a successful flower business in Brisbane with his wife.

30. VICTOR TRUMPER

Victor Thomas Trumper, b. 2 November 1877, probably in Sydney; d. 28 June 1915, Sydney

First-class: 16,939 runs (44.57) 64 wickets (31.37) and 171 catches
Tests (48): 3,163 runs (39.04), eight wickets (39.62) and 31 catches

Some of Victor Trumper's greatness has to be taken on trust because he died at the age of 38, making headline news far away in England even at the height of the First World War. His figures are not as remarkable as those of a few others, even allowing for the difficulties of the uncovered and often bumpy pitches on which he played. They are almost identical, of example, to those of Clem Hill, the greatest Australian left-hander of the time. Nevertheless, so many of his contemporaries pronounced Trumper the finest batsman that they have to be believed.

Pelham Warner's verdict was clear:

No one ever played so naturally. He had grace, ease, style, power and a quickness of foot both in jumping out and getting back. He had every known stroke and one or two of his own. When set on a good wicket it seemed impossible to place a field for him. He was somewhat lightly built, but his sense of timing was so perfect that he hit the ball tremendously hard.

Jack Fingleton also quoted the words of his club captain in Sydney, the renowned wicket-keeper Hanson Carter: 'If you want to try to classify the great batsmen in the game put Victor Trumper way up there – on his own – and then you can begin to talk about the rest.' Perhaps another contemporary, Leslie Poidevin, summed it up when he said: 'His best was the best.'

It was on bad pitches that he proved his greatness but he was quite prepared to enjoy himself on good ones. On his first visit to England in 1899, when he scored 135 not out in his second Test match, at Lord's, he made a chanceless 300 not out in six hours and twenty minutes against Sussex. He became a great favourite of English crowds on three further tours, scoring 2,570 runs, 956 more than anyone else, in the wet summer of 1902. He scored eleven centuries on the trip and his 104 on the drying pitch at Old Trafford, when England lost by three runs, became part of cricket legend. He dominated the 1910-11 series against South Africa, averaging 94, including 214 not out at Adelaide.

The beauty of his character matched that of his batting. At Sydney in the first Test of the 1903-04 series against England he made 185 not out with a new bat that he had apparently picked, untested, from the shelves of his own sports shop. An admirer came into the shop the following week, asked first if he could see the bat and then, falteringly, whether Trumper might be prepared to part with it, knowing that a considerable mark-up for a potentially priceless artefact would only be reasonable. What, then, might be the price? 'Well,' said Trumper, 'it cost two pounds, five shillings new ... so let's say two pounds.'

29. ALEC BEDSER

Sir Alec Victor Bedser, b. 4 July 1918, Reading

First-class: 5,735 runs (14.51), 1,924 wickets (20.41) and 290 catches
Tests (51): 714 runs (12.75), 236 wickets (24.89) and 26 catches

The name A.V. Bedser was a familiar and essential entry on scorecards at the Oval, and all the main grounds of England and Australia, for a decade after the Second World War. The 'V' stood for Victor and it was appropriate. Bedser was indomitable, an oak tree among saplings in England teams in those years of post-war austerity and gradual recovery.

Until the arrival of the Truemans and Stathams he was the pillar, and built like one too. Tall and broad, almost a human replica of one of the mighty trees that he and his twin brother Eric used to fell in the winter to keep themselves fit and strong, he loved bowling and would do it all day if his captain asked or required it.

He liked his wicket-keepers to stand up to the stumps, and in Godfrey Evans for England and Arthur McIntyre for Surrey he had two men good enough to do it. Bedser had a sturdy, classical action

after a run-up long enough only to give him the momentum to release the ball from a high position after a vigorous turn of the upper body. That gave his medium- to fast-medium-paced bowling kick off the pitch, allowing little margin for batsmen's error when it moved through the air or off the seam, which invariably it did.

It was propelled by a huge right hand that cut and spun the ball, very much in the tradition of Sydney Barnes. His stock ball swung in to right-handers, but increasingly they came to fear the Bedser leg-cutter that had dumbfounded a well-set Don Bradman on the easiest of Adelaide pitches in 1946-47.

He took 100 wickets in eleven seasons, helping Surrey to their record run of Championship titles from 1952 to 1958. His Test career started with eleven wickets in each of his first two Tests, against India in 1946. His sixteen wickets in the first one-sided post-war series in Australia were costly, at 54 runs each, but the next time he went there, four years later, he took 30 at sixteen and when the Ashes were regained in 1953 he was in his pomp. He took 39 wickets at seventeen in the five Tests, including fourteen for 99 at Trent Bridge.

His standards remained admirably high until, suffering from shingles, he was left out by Len Hutton after the defeat at Brisbane in the first Test of 1954-55. It ended a conscientious career during which his catching had been utterly reliable and his wooden but determined batting occasionally useful, notably against Australia at Headingley in 1948 when he went in as a night-watchman and scored 79.

Bedser served as an England selector for 23 years, and as chairman of the committee from 1969 until 1981. He was president of Surrey in 1987. His character was loyal, steadfast and dutiful. He reached the age of 90 in 2008, no longer able to play golf because, as he would say, 'my knees are b......d' but battling on despite the loss of Eric, his hitherto inseparable twin, and the female companion who had brightened his old age. Nothing, though, would alter his disillusionment with the modern game and especially with bowlers who failed to put the ball on a length. Some of cricket's essentials, he knew, will survive all trends and changes.

28. BARRY RICHARDS

Barry Anderson Richards, b. 21 July 1945, Durban

First-class: 28,358 runs (54.75), 77 wickets (37.48) and 367 catches
Tests (4): 508 runs (72.57), one wicket (26) and three catches

If Barry Richards was often a little careless with his talent, it was understandable because he apparently found cricket ridiculously easy. In the early 1970s he was the best batsman in the world and he would no doubt have remained so had not South Africa's isolation from world sport forced him to ply his trade, prosperously but often without fulfillment, as an itinerant mercenary on a lower plane, mainly for Hampshire and Natal.

His only Test series consisted of four matches for South Africa against Australia in 1969-70, when he reached the first of his two hundreds in his second Test off 116 balls in the over after lunch at Kingsmead. His eventual 140 came from 164 balls. His 508 runs in four matches helped South Africa to their only 100 per cent record in 81 years of Test cricket.

He played for South Australia in one prolific season in 1970-71, making 356, 325 of them in one six-hour day, against Western Australia in Perth. All but one of the six bowlers pitted against him in that match played Test cricket and three of them – Dennis Lillee, Graham McKenzie and Tony Lock – were from the top drawer. Richards also savaged John Snow that Australian summer while making a double century against the MCC touring team. He averaged 109 over the season and piloted South Australia to the Sheffield Shield title.

Other challenges included playing for the Rest of the World side in the 1970 series in England that would otherwise have been a South African tour, and, in contests that fully tested his mettle, for another World XI against most of the best of the Australians and

West Indians in World Series Cricket in 1978-80. From 1981 to 1984 he represented South Africa in unofficial matches against English and West Indies elevens.

Hooked by cricket from a young age in Durban, Richards went to England as captain of the South African Schools side in 1963, played for a month for Gloucestershire two years later and for Hampshire from 1968 to 1978, forming with Gordon Greenidge the most exciting opening partnership in county cricket.

Tallish and sparely built, with curly hair and distinctive buck teeth, Richards was the perfect model for any batsman. The time that he had to size up the length and direction of each ball was uncanny. Always balanced and unhurried, he never had to reach for the ball but played it under his eyes, preferring the straight-batted shots to those played square of the wicket but capable, it seemed, of playing any shot to any ball, not least the hook against the quickest bowling. Batting without a helmet in the bouncer-happy World Series matches, he scored two centuries in the 'Supertests' after which Lillee called him the 'personification of batting perfection'.

In his first season for Hampshire he scored 2,395 runs during a wet summer, and his many remarkable performances for the county in ensuing years included an innings of 240 against Warwickshire in 1973, when Hampshire's next highest scorer made 56. His double century against Nottinghamshire at Trent Bridge in 1974 came in a game in which only two other players scored more than 30. In the same season he made 189 out of a total of 249 for six against MCC at Lord's.

Throughout his career he made slip catching look even easier than batting, and was capable of valuable spells as an off-spin bowler. He married an Australian squash champion from Perth. Since retirement he has divided his time between business, cricket administration in Australia and television and radio commentary.

27. F.R. SPOFFORTH

Frederick Robert Spofforth, b. 9 September 1853, Balmain, New South Wales; d. 4 June 1926, Long Ditton, Surrey

First-class: 1,928 runs (9.88), 853 wickets (14.95) and 83 catches
Tests (18): 217 runs (9.43), 94 wickets (18.41) and eleven catches

'The Demon' Spofforth was the first legendary bowler of the Test match era, a tall, spare, strong and forbidding Australian fast bowler with a big moustache who did more than anyone to make Englishmen appreciate that the 'colonials' not only had to be taken seriously, but might actually be superior.

Six foot three, he ran in fast from nine paces and leapt menacingly, with his left arm high in front of his face, before delivering the ball with a vigorous turn of the body and full follow-through. George Giffen thought that he simply frightened many opponents out by the sheer 'devilry' of his appearance, and 'Plum' Warner spoke of his hooked nose, piercing eyes and concentrated aggression.

He was a sprinter who ran 100 yards in 10.2 seconds in 1881, a New South Wales record. Like many of the great fast bowlers, he started as a tearaway but developed craft and changes of pace. He studied and practised three kinds of what he called 'swerve': out, in and 'vertical', the latter a mixture of top spin and back spin, achieved by flicking his fingers down the (then very flat) seam of the ball as he bowled it. He controlled his pace by gripping the ball more or less tightly, sometimes holding on to only a part of it.

As a twenty-year-old he clean-bowled seven batsmen in taking nine for ten against Sydney University, before playing for New South Wales from 1874. He would have played in the first ever Test in Melbourne, but withdrew because Jack Blackham was chosen as wicket-keeper ahead of the New South Wales wicket-keeper, Billy Murdoch. He made up for lost time when he first went to England in 1878, bowling almost twice as many overs as anyone else and taking double the

number of any other bowler's wickets. At Lord's in May he famously bowled W.G. Grace for a duck in taking six for four and five for sixteen as MCC were routed in a day.

He made four more tours to England in the 1880s and later appeared for Derbyshire for three seasons starting in 1889, taking fifteen wickets in one match against Yorkshire, whence his father, a banker, had originally emigrated to Australia.

The Ashes legend emanates from the reaction to Australia's victory at the Oval in 1882, when 'the Demon' took fourteen for 90. England had needed only 85 to win but Spofforth famously told his colleagues in the dressing room: 'This thing can be done.' It did not seem so when, on a chilly August afternoon, England reached fifteen for no wicket, then 30 for one and 51 for two, leaving only 34 to get with Grace still in. But he was fourth out, caught at mid-off from a slower ball by Harry Boyle. At one point, seventeen overs passed with only a single run scored. Eventually 'the thing' – Australia's first win in a Test in England – was achieved by seven runs, Spofforth bowling unchanged from the Vauxhall end for figures of seven for 46 from 36 overs and three balls.

In the eleven-a-side games in England he took 123 wickets at 11.37 in 1878, 118 at 12.12 in 1880 and 216 at 12.23 in 1884. The game was played at a different speed on very different pitches compared to the present day, but these were the performances of a great and highly original bowler. He eventually settled in England, becoming a director of his father-in-law's tea company and a wealthy man.

26. SUNIL GAVASKAR

Sunil Manohar Gavaskar, b. 10 July 1949, Bombay

First-class: 25,834 runs (51.46), 22 wickets (56.36) and 293 catches
Tests (125): 10,122 runs (51.12), one wicket (206.00) and 108 catches

One-day internationals (108): 392 runs (35.15), 25 wickets (25.00) and 22 catches

All the elements of a great batsman – instant reflexes, quick footwork, courage, limitless concentration and, above all, a model technique – made Sunil Gavaskar the best of the various 'little masters' from the Indian subcontinent until Sachin Tendulkar exceeded even his own remarkable achievements. Gavaskar was the first batsman to exceed 10,000 Test runs, and his 34 Test centuries had set a new yardstick by the time that he retired in 1988.

A little under five foot five inches, but compact and strong, Gavaskar could play every shot in the textbook with his head always over the ball. He was always an opening batsman, despite his watertight defence, more often prepared to take control in the middle than, for example, Hanif Mohammad, who had equal patience and ability; and less inclined to be rash than other diminutive batsmen of great talent, like the brilliant Aravinda de Silva or his own teammate Gundappa Vishwanath. Only a certain moodiness limited him, most notably when in the first match of the 1975 Prudential World Cup he batted through the 60 overs of India's innings for 36 not out.

Born into the Marathi middle class of Bombay, Gavaskar learned his technique in junior cricket in Bombay, often on poor pitches on the Maidaan. As Mihir Bose later observed, he mixed a Hindu work ethic with discipline from his Jesuit education at St Xavier's School and College and he pursued success on the cricket field, and its financial rewards, with an open ambition. His father was a keen cricketer and his mother's uncle, M.K. Mantri, had kept wicket for India. His sister married Gundappa Vishwanath and his own son, Rohan (after Rohan Kanhai), has played in one-day internationals for India.

Sunil started as he went on. In his first Test series in 1970-71 he scored 774 runs, despite having missed the first Test because of an infected fingernail. He scored 65 and 67 not out in his first match, when India beat the West Indies for the first time, centuries in the next two Tests and, in the final match, 124 out of India's first innings

total of 360 at Port of Spain. It was a six-day match because the series was still open. The West Indies responded with 526, so India's first series win in the Caribbean was in jeopardy when, despite severe toothache for which he refused to take painkillers, he scored 220. It took his average to 154.8, a record for anyone's maiden series, and one of many he was to break.

Proving his ability to play well in any conditions, he scored 101 and 58 in Indian totals of 246 and 182 on a seaming pitch and in cold weather at Old Trafford in 1974. In Australia in 1977-78 he scored centuries in the first three Tests, at Brisbane, Perth and Melbourne. He scored 1,004 runs in his nine Tests in 1978, including 447 at an average of 89 against Pakistan. He was rewarded with the captaincy of India for the first time in the home series against the West Indies in 1978-79, scoring 732 runs and four more hundreds in the six Tests, but was then relieved of the leadership in England in 1979 where he nevertheless produced his masterpiece, a flawless eight-hour innings of 221 at the Oval in the fourth innings. It came close to winning a game in which India had seemed doomed.

He regained the captaincy and led with authority, but the storms that sometimes brewed beneath an exterior of great charm and dignity emerged occasionally. Furious at being given out LBW in the Melbourne Test in 1980-81 he ordered his opening partner, Chetan Chauhan, to walk off with him, intending that India should forfeit the match in protest. He then apologised, the game was resumed and India won. His record 30th Test century came against the West Indies at Madras in 1983-84 – he went on to make 236 – and he showed his mastery to the end, making a century at Lord's, one thing that had hitherto eluded him, in the MCC bicentenary match in 1987.

Such has been Gavaskar's fame in India that he still cannot go anywhere without being surrounded by worshippers eager just to touch him. In 2001 a young batsman about to play his first Test sought an audience, and took his leave by kissing the demigod's feet.

25. RICHARD HADLEE

Sir Richard John Hadlee, b. 3 July 1951, Christchurch, New Zealand

First-class: 12,052 runs (27.16), 1,490 wickets (18.11) and 198 catches
Tests (86): 3,124 runs (27.16), 431 wickets (22.29) and 39 catches
One-day internationals (115): 1,751 runs (21.62), 158 wickets (21.56)
and 27 catches

New Zealand has never had a bowler as incisive as Richard Hadlee. A waspish fast-medium bowler of surgical precision with a shrewd, analytical mind, he produced genuinely quick balls when necessary, and by utter dedication to his craft acquired perfect control once he had honed the rambling action of his fast-bowling youth.

Six foot tall, lean, hard and very fit, he cut his run-up to no more than fifteen purposeful paces. His sideways-on action generated lift and sufficient out- or in-swing for his purposes, but his secret was a rigid wrist behind the ball that ensured that it landed on the seam every time, cutting this way or that. He took five or more wickets 36 times in Test cricket, and played many a swashbuckling innings as a hard-driving left-hander in the middle order.

Generally, he liked to stay inside the line of the fastest bowling and thrash it through the covers when he could. The first of his two Test hundreds came from only 92 balls against the West Indies at Christchurch in 1978-79, in a series in which he also took nineteen wickets at nineteen runs each. For Nottinghamshire, through years of determined service that led to two Championships, he became the first man to do the double since Fred Titmus in 1967, when in 1984 he scored 1,179 runs at 51.26 and took 117 wickets at fourteen. He reached 100 off 93 balls against Middlesex at Lord's, and went on to a score of 210 not out.

Largely through Hadlee's efforts and those of New Zealand's most accomplished Test batsman, Martin Crowe, they were able to beat all

the other Test nations at least once during the period between 1979 and 1984.

Richard was the fourth son of New Zealand's popular captain in England on the 1949 tour, Walter Hadlee. With his brothers Dayle, also a Test fast bowler, and Barry, he was a member of the New Zealand team in the first of the World Cups in England, in 1975. He had already toured England in 1973, and when he next confronted them in 1978 he was the spearhead of an attack that beat them for the first time, at Wellington. Hadlee took ten wickets for 100 in the match, including six for 26 to shatter their second innings for 64.

With seven wickets he had also had a strong hand in New Zealand's maiden victory over Australia on his home ground, Lancaster Park in Christchurch, in 1974. He took seven for 23 against India at Wellington in 1975-76. On any ground where there was some juice in the pitch, he was always a potential match-winner.

The peak of many fine performances at home and away against Australia came in 1985-86 when he took 33 wickets at 12.15 in the three-Test series, including nine for 52 and six for 71 at Brisbane, a near-perfect exhibition topped by an innings of 54 to ensure a satisfying victory. New Zealand won a series in England for the first time in 1986, Hadlee taking nineteen wickets at twenty runs each. In the decisive match at his second home, Trent Bridge, he took ten for 140 and made an aggressive 68. For Nottinghamshire, in his final season of 1987, he scored 1,111 runs and took 97 wickets as the Championship was won again.

If that was a high point, so was the moment in 1990 when he became the first bowler in Test cricket to take 400 wickets, achieving this in only his 79th game, in his home city of Christchurch. Having been awarded an MBE for services to cricket in 1980, he was knighted in 1990 during his final tour to England.

24. BRIAN LARA

Brian Charles Lara, b. 2 May 1969, Santa Cruz, Trinidad

First-class: 22,156 runs (51.88), four wickets (104.00) and 320 catches
Tests (131): 11,953 runs (52.88) and 164 catches
One-day internationals (299): 10,405 runs (40.48), four wickets (15.25)
and 120 catches

Brian Lara was at once a dazzling star and a relentless record-breaker. His misfortune was to be the outstanding West Indies player at a time when their period of unrelenting success had ended. He was among the best of all batsmen in any era and of any country. In the West Indies he continued a line of genius started by George Headley and maintained by Walcott, Weekes, Worrell, Sobers and Richards.

Lara's special gift was to combine remorseless efficiency with an ability to be constantly entertaining. Even in defence his stylish left-handed batting was fascinating, perhaps because of the extraordinary fullness and speed of his backlift, which threatened an attacking shot to every ball.

He was on the winning team in only 32 of his 131 Tests and the West Indies actually won 13 per cent more games – ten out of 27 – when he was not playing. That he started his career just as they were running out of fast bowlers, following nearly twenty years when their bowling prowess made it so much easier for the likes of Richards, is one of the reasons that he was long the subject of controversy and gossip. In stronger teams the limelight would not have been so constantly upon him, although it was in his three periods as captain that it burned most brightly and, despite a sunny outward mien, uncomfortably. Like Sobers before him he was not sufficiently shrewd, sympathetic or responsible to be a good team captain.

He played 131 Test matches, starting in Lahore in 1990-91. He had been made to wait for his first game in a strong side, despite the fact that everyone had known of his prodigious talent since the little

left-hander from Santa Cruz in Trinidad began to score centuries in youth tournaments. He went on to score 34 for the West Indies and retired in 2007 with more Test runs than any other man, although he would eventually be overtaken by Sachin Tendulkar.

He retired, too, with the record for the highest individual Test score, 400 not out at the St John's Recreation Ground in Antigua against England in 2004, and the highest in first-class cricket, 501 not out for Warwickshire against Durham at Edgbaston when he hit 62 fours and ten sixes and made his runs from only 427 balls. Chris Scott, Durham's wicket-keeper, had dropped the only chance Lara offered, early in this phenomenal display of brilliance. 'I bet he goes on to make a hundred now,' he said to the nearest slip.

I saw every run of his 400, the last 125 or so of his 501 and every one too of his 375 against England in Antigua in 1993-94, the innings which first broke the Sobers record of 365 not out. Nothing disturbed the even tenor of his way during these performances. He never looked like getting out yet he was never dull. You could only marvel at the full back lift, the timing, the placement, the wristy command and hidden ruthlessness with which he dominated attacks.

Glenn McGrath, who dismissed him fifteen times in Tests, was probably the only bowler who got the better of him. It was in McGrath's home state, at Sydney, that Lara first announced his genius beyond question when he made 277 in 1992-93 in only his ninth Test innings. Against Australia, too, he played perhaps his greatest innings, the 153 not out that enabled the West Indies, under his captaincy, to score more than 400 in the fourth innings to win the Bridgetown Test against long odds in 1999.

In that series he also scored a double hundred at Kingston and another century at St John's. Throughout his career, dazzling bursts of form were far more frequent than periods of struggle. He averaged 51 overall in 31 Tests against Australia, and 62 in 30 against England. He made sixteen centuries against those two countries alone. Only against India were his figures anything like modest: despite a mastery of spin based on twinkling footwork, he averaged only 34 in his seventeen Tests against them. But like all opponents they felt the power of his blade in limited-over games. He scored nineteen one-day-international hundreds.

23. BILL O'REILLY

William Joseph O'Reilly, b. 20 December 1905, White Cliffs, New South Wales; d. 6 October 1992, Sydney

First-class: 1,655 runs (13.13), 774 wickets (16.60) and 65 catches
Tests (27): 410 runs (12.81), 144 wickets (22.59) and seven catches

William Joseph O'Reilly was well named 'Tiger'. In a career that would have been still more illustrious but for the Second World War, he hunted batsmen with a fire that burnt bright. Fiercely independent, his method was all his own. A heaving action, remorseless accuracy and his own mixture of leg-breaks and googlies made him the most dangerous bowler in the world through the 1930s, when most of the headlines were being made by record-breaking batsmen.

Don Bradman, chief among them, had been bowled round his legs at the age of seventeen by O'Reilly during a game in the New South Wales 'bush' at Wingello in 1926. (Bradman was resuming his innings having made a double hundred in the first leg of the two-day game at Bowral.) They developed a mutual respect, but it took time and they were never friends. Bradman, eventually to judge him the greatest bowler he played with or against, wrote O'Reilly off in 1930 as someone who could 'make the ball turn both ways but never achieved any outstanding success on turf pitches'.

He was not alone in misjudging the tall, strong schoolmaster whose wrist spin was bowled at medium pace after a long, lumbering run-up, like a ship lunging through a rough sea. With a contorted face and flailing arms, he kept a tight grip on the ball with long, strong fingers and then stooped as he delivered the ball. The other side of the coin was that the final sweep of his arm was a full one and, as Ian Peebles observed, 'the general gusto of his performance made it very difficult to gauge his pace from his hand'.

As he matured he mixed his leg-break with two top spinners and a loopier, high-bouncing googly. His first efforts for New South Wales

in 1927-28 were modest, but he was concentrating on his career as a teacher, and moved to a new job at Griffith where he worked on his game but refused to change his action. He returned to Sydney late in 1930 and in 1931-32, following success in Grade cricket, he returned to take 25 wickets in five games for the state. Picked for the last two Tests of that season against South Africa, he had the first of many outstanding series against England the following year, taking 27 wickets at 27 in the 'Bodyline' series.

In England in 1934 he and Clarrie Grimmett formed a match-winning combination. At Nottingham O'Reilly took eleven for 139, and at Old Trafford he provided a typical thrust by getting out Walters, Wyatt and Hammond in four balls. On the tour to South Africa in 1935-36 he took 95 wickets at thirteen runs each, and in England in 1938 he took more than 100 wickets on the tour a second time, including a decisive ten for 122 at Headingley when he dismissed Walter Hammond first ball with his googly.

In fifteen seasons of club cricket, O'Reilly took 921 wickets at an average below ten. He was generous in sharing his knowledge with other bowlers. Even during his many years in the press box after retirement he was always on their side against batsmen, even when the batsmen were Aussies, and especially if the bowler was a wrist-spinner. I remember his incandescence at the failure of the Pakistan captain to set fields appropriate to the wiles of Abdul Qadir. His speech was candid, and there was often a scowl on the face of the Tiger, but he had a big heart, an astute mind and a deep enthusiasm for cricket.

22. F.S. TRUEMAN

Frederick Sewards Trueman, b. 6 February 1931, Stainton, Yorkshire; d. 6 July 2006, Yorkshire

First-class: 9,231 runs (15.56), 2,304 wickets (18.29) and 439 catches
Tests (67): 981 runs (13.81), 307 wickets (21.57) and 64 catches

Both a great bowler and a born entertainer, with a quick wit, long memory and wonderful gift for anecdote, Fred Trueman was a national treasure. Sadly he could never quite accept that he was, nor rid himself of the notion that he was fighting unseen hostile forces emanating from the British establishment, often imagined and usually associated with MCC, most of whose members loved him. It suited him to play the role of working-class hero.

For all the bluster that accompanied his fast bowling, on and off the field, the essence of his success was a physique of great strength and a superb action. The son of a coal miner, he had legs as thick as an elephant's, broad shoulders and beam, a deep chest, and a bowling action that built momentum like a gathering storm. The first bowler in history to take 300 Test wickets, in 1964, he had everything needed to be a great fast bowler. The magnificent rhythm and coordination of his delivery, following a long final stride during which his head was perfectly level as he looked over his left shoulder before releasing the ball, gave him natural speed. To this he added the necessary mental aggression.

Most of his wickets were the product of consistent late out-swing, leading to catches in the slips or at the wicket. In his youth especially he was also happy to pepper the batsmen with bouncers. He greatly enjoyed the epithet 'Fiery Fred' that soon became familiar in the popular press after his first appearance for Yorkshire in 1949. Later he developed great craft that enabled him to bowl opponents out with off cutters or by changing his angle of delivery, but he would trade on his hostility against any opponent who looked timorous, sometimes softening them up further by going into their dressing-room to say how much he was looking forward to getting them out; and telling them how he would do it.

There was something of Emily Brontë's Heathcliff in his appearance. Craggy-faced and with bushy eyebrows, a mane of dark hair would flop forward as he bowled and be tossed back with a flick of the head as he walked back, full of intent, rolling up the sleeve of the right arm that would invariably have been loosened by the vigour of his delivery.

Both his speed and his visible belligerence were too much for the Indians in his first Test series in 1952. He took 24 wickets in three

Tests, including seven at Leeds, when, sensationally, four India wickets fell before the first run was scored in their second innings, three of them to Trueman. He followed up with eight for 31 in the first innings at Old Trafford.

India's number three that day, H.R. Adhikari (caught Graveney bowled Trueman 0), came back to England many summers later as Colonel Adhikari, manager of another Indian touring team. 'Nice to see you again, Colonel,' said Fred on being reintroduced. 'And good to see you've got some colour back.'

National service in the RAF interrupted his career, and the rough edges evident on his first MCC tour in the West Indies in 1953-54 led to his surprising omission from Len Hutton's side in Australia the following winter, despite his having taken 124 wickets at sixteen in the intervening summer. Frank Tyson, who was even faster, kept him out of the side and by 1957, five years after his extraordinary debut, he had only played seven Tests. That year, however, he started a six-year association with Brian Statham that became the most productive in the world.

For ten consecutive seasons between 1957 and 1966 he took at least 100 wickets, including 175 at 13.98 in 1960. In the first eight months of that year he played ten Tests and took 46 wickets. The following year at Headingley he slowed his pace to bowl off-cutters in the third Test against Australia, and dismissed five prime batsmen without conceding a run. He took eleven for 88 in the match and England won.

Yorkshire won six Championships during his career, and he captained them to victory against virtually the Australia Test side at Bramall Lane in 1968, one of his proudest moments. He would no doubt have made a success of more regular captaincy in his maturity. He was, throughout his career, a useful batsman who liked to give the ball a hearty biff and a fine fielder anywhere, not least at short-leg to spin bowlers.

In retirement he was a popular member of the *Test Match Special* team of radio commentators, intolerant of modest play or players but brilliant when the rain was falling and he could indulge his memory. For a time he was also a stand-up comic and for much longer a ribald after-dinner speaker. In 1972 he was persuaded by Derbyshire to play some limited-overs cricket.

21. DENIS COMPTON

Denis Charles Scott Compton, b. 23 May 1918, Hendon, Middlesex

First-class: 38,942 runs (51.85), 622 wickets (32.27) and 416 catches
Tests (78): 5,807 runs (50.06), 25 wickets (56.40) and 49 catches

Denis Compton had the status in English national life of David Beckham in more recent times. Especially as a consequence of his golden summer in 1947 he became a household name, a public hero. Everybody knew who he was, and for sports-minded schoolboys of the time he was an idol.

Compton was carefree, warm-hearted, charming and vague. He had a genius for batting and it came to the fore at a propitious time, just as the exigencies of 1939-45 were starting to ease. There was a nostalgia for the traditions that the hardships and tragedies of wartime had pushed into the background; county cricket was one of them. In a hot summer Compton and his Middlesex 'twin', Bill Edrich, put a long succession of bowling attacks to the sword, making Lord's their personal playground. The South African touring team was unwillingly but resignedly compliant in their great adventure. Of his 3,816 runs in the season, Compton scored 753 against them in the five Tests. He scored eighteen hundreds, still and perhaps forever a first-class record. With his confidence high and nothing to lose, he also took 73 wickets at 28 runs each that season with his chinamen and googlies.

His batting was adventurous – as his teammate John Warr wrote, it had 'a poetic quality mixed with the spirit of the eternal schoolboy' – but it was based on a sound technique. As with all the great batsmen, he played the ball from beneath his eyes, carried always to the right position by quicksilver footwork. Cover-drives stroked into gaps by instinct and late guidance from the wrists were his most pleasing shots, but his most famous was the sweep. Football on the wing for

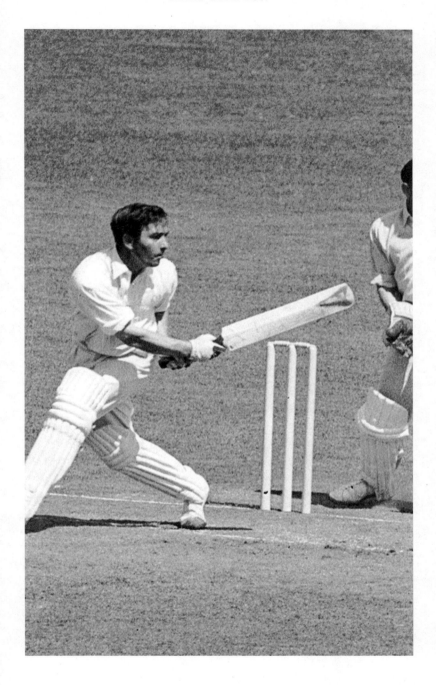

Arsenal, and in fourteen wartime internationals for England, must have helped his mobility, although it also left him the legacy of a knee injury which blighted his later seasons as a cricketer. The 'Compton knee' became a national talking point.

He first appeared for Middlesex in 1936 as a slow left-arm (then orthodox) bowler but made 1,000 runs in a season for the first time the following year, and made 65 in his first Test against New Zealand before being run out. He remained an erratic runner. In his next Test, the first at Trent Bridge against Australia, he scored a century, as did Len Hutton, by whom he was eclipsed later that season but with whom he was to share the main burden of keeping England's batting together against stronger Australian sides after the war. In 1946-47 he made 459 in the Ashes series at 51, and in 1948 562 runs at 62.

Perhaps the last of his wholly uninhibited innings was one of 300 in three hours, the fastest triple hundred ever scored, for MCC against North-East Transvaal at Benoni in 1948-49. Handicapped afterwards by knee pain, he seldom played so magically again, although the first Pakistan touring team in 1954 got some idea of his talent when he made 278 in 290 minutes in the second Test at Trent Bridge.

After an operation to remove his right kneecap, he returned for the last Test against Australia to score 94 in the final Test in 1956. I was there. Memories are hazy of the innings itself but the realisation that it was his last Test left an indelible impression on an eleven-year-old mind, because all the adults were talking about it. He finished with 123 hundreds, seventeen in Tests.

Compton's elder brother, Leslie, also played for Arsenal and Middlesex. Denis, never short of female company, married three times. His sons were good school cricketers and one of his grandsons has played for Middlesex.

20. GEORGE HEADLEY

George Alphonso Headley, b. 30 May 1909, Panama; d. 30 November 1983, Jamaica

First-class: 9,921 runs (69.86), 51 wickets (36.11) and 76 catches
Tests (22): 2,190 runs (60.83), and fourteen catches

For almost the whole of his career, observed C.L.R. James, George Headley went in to bat at number three for the West Indies knowing that if he failed they would probably be bowled out for 150. In fifteen of his 35 Test innings he was his team's top scorer. In eleven of them he made at least a third of the runs and in three of them more than half. In the 1930s he averaged a hundred every other Test he played. He was known as the black Bradman, but he certainly had less support.

His father, from Barbados, went to Panama to help build the canal. His mother was Jamaican. George was born in Panama and did not go to school in Jamaica until he had also spent four years in Cuba, where his parents had moved in search of further work. In Kingston, having shown his natural talent at school, he joined the St Catherine Club and at the age of eighteen played for Jamaica for the first time against Lionel Tennyson's English touring team. He scored 71, 211 out of 348 and 71 again despite which, somehow, he was overlooked for the tour of England in 1928. Lesser and whiter players were preferred, and England won all three Tests.

Hitherto representatives of the black working class had mainly been fast bowlers, but Headley was allowed to bat at three against England in 1929-30, and in his first Test in Bridgetown he obliged with 21 and 176 in a drawn match. At Georgetown in the third Test he scored centuries in each innings to inspire the first West Indies Test victory. The first Test batsman to make three hundreds before his 21st birthday, he added a fourth – 223, no less – in his fourth match,

at Sabina Park, whereupon the local legend became a batsman of far wider fame.

Much was made of the comparison with Bradman on the first West Indies tour of Australia. He took time to counter Clarrie Grimmett's unfamiliar leg-spin, but scored two hundreds in the Tests and over 1,000 runs on the tour. Confronted by a second touring team under Lord Tennyson in 1931-2 he scored 344 not out for Jamaica, and in England in 1933 he made seven more centuries, including 169 not out in the Manchester Test. His 485 runs in the home series against England in 1934-35 were scored at an average of 97, and before the war virtually ended his career he made one more tour of England, averaging 72 and making 100 in each innings of the Lord's Test.

Headley was a quiet master of his art. His style, said R.C. Robertson-Glasgow, was suited by bowling pitched short of a length. 'He delights in hooking, in delayed deflections to leg and in cutting square and late. In these arts he has no living superior.'

Like Bradman in the context of Australia's breaking free from colonial status, Headley's success, and the dignity with which he behaved, was symbolic of the black man's aspirations towards equal status with whites in what remained a class- and colour-conscious world, in the Caribbean as everywhere else. Sir Pelham Warner, Trinidad-born, had invited Learie Constantine to captain the Dominions side at Lord's in 1945, but the moment when Headley led the West Indies team out at Bridgetown in January 1948 was one of great political significance: he was the first black man to captain the West Indies in a Test.

His son, Ron, although playing most of his cricket for Worcestershire, won two Test caps for the West Indies and his grandson, Dean, bowled fast for England with great promise until injuries forced early retirement.

19. DENNIS LILLEE

Dennis Keith Lillee, b. 18 July 1949, Perth, Western Australia

First-class: 2,377 runs (13.90), 882 wickets (23.46) and 67 catches
Tests (70): 905 runs (13.71), 355 wickets (23.92) and 23 catches
One-day internationals (63): 240 runs (9.23), 103 wickets (20.82) and ten
catches

There can never have been so spectacular a fast bowler as Dennis Lillee, nor one so unremittingly hostile. When his fire was stoked, even his smile seemed more like a sneer.

Tall, broad-shouldered and sparely strong, he kept his dark hair long, restraining it with a bandana rather than letting the barber get at it. He ran at full pelt towards the climax of his action, not so much with purpose as with a deadly menace. The final delivery after an explosive leap was magnificent from a distance, but daunting from the batsman's viewpoint nineteen yards away.

All this would have counted for little had he been no more than a blusterer but he also bowled with great speed and accuracy, swinging the new ball away late from the right-handers. Later in his career, when back and knee injuries restricted his pace, he developed outstanding craft. He almost always extracted more bounce from pitches than his rivals, and 95 of his Test wickets were caught by his outstanding wicket-keeping contemporary from Western Australia, Rod Marsh.

Success in his home town of Perth was rewarded by his selection for the last two Tests of the 1970-71 series against England at the age of 21. He took five wickets in his first innings. After a summer in league cricket in England to further his bowling education, he produced an astonishing performance in December 1971 against a powerful Rest of the World team that included Gavaskar, Kanhai,

Zaheer Abbas, Clive Lloyd, Tony Greig and Gary Sobers. Bowling with Perth's famous wind from Freemantle behind him, Lillee took eight of the nine wickets to fall to bowlers, six of them for no runs. In his three representative matches in the unofficial Test series he took 24 wickets at twenty, figures that, like later outstanding ones in World Series cricket, do not count in his Test record.

In England in 1972 he was exceptional, taking 31 Test wickets at seventeen. He had learned a leg-cutter from John Snow and shortened his original, rather ragged run-up on the advice of Ray Lindwall. He broke down with stress fractures in his back in the West Indies, missing a year's cricket, but put himself through a punishing routine to return to full fitness in 1974-75, forming a devastating opening partnership with Jeff Thomson. Together they were the enforcers in winning series at home against England, when Lillee took 25 wickets, and the West Indies the following season when he claimed another 27. In between, he was the leading bowler in England in 1975, with 21 Test wickets at 21. Having been too good for Pakistan and New Zealand in 1976-77 he rose to the great occasion of the centenary Test, taking six for 26 on a drying pitch in the first innings and then five for 129 on a comfortable one in the second.

He took 79 wickets at 23 in the 'Supertests' of World Series Cricket during the two-year schism in the world game, out-bowling Andy Roberts and Michael Holding. By sheer technical skill, determination and cunning he remained the best fast bowler in the world until his retirement, taking 85 Test wickets at only twenty runs each in 1981, including 39 in the Ashes series in England, despite suffering a virus for much of the tour. Only in Pakistan, where the dead-slow pitches nullified even his inventiveness, did he fail, taking only three wickets for 303. He had ample revenge against Pakistan on bouncier pitches at home.

Lillee was a popular hero in Australia, often urged on by adoring chants of 'Lil-leee, Lil-leee'. The bigger the crowd, the greater the mutual admiration. But sometimes the 'larrikin' pushed his luck. He showed impudence in asking the Queen for her autograph when the teams were presented to her during the centenary Test at Melbourne (she was amused), arrogance when using an aluminium bat in a marketing ploy during the Perth Test in 1979-80, holding up play for ten minutes, and ill temper when aiming a public kick at Pakistan's provocative captain, Javed Miandad, again at Perth.

With Lillee, such behaviour went only skin deep. He hated any pomposity but his essential character was generous and gregarious. He became the most eagerly followed fast bowling coach, especially in India where his work during annual sponsored sessions at the Pace Academy in Madras had much to do with the production of several outstanding Indian fast bowlers.

18. IAN BOTHAM

Sir Ian Terence Botham, b. 24 November 1955, Heswell, Cheshire

First-class: 19,399 runs (33.97), 1,172 wickets (27.22) and 354 catches
Tests (102): 5,200 runs (33.54), 383 wickets (28.40) and 120 catches.
One-day internationals (116): 2,113 runs (23.22), 145 wickets (28.54)
and 36 catches

Ian Botham assured himself of immortality by transforming the 1981 Ashes series from a personal catastrophe into an amazing triumph. One of the four great all-rounders of the 1980s – Imran Khan, Kapil Dev and Richard Hadlee being the others – he would always vie with Walter Hammond for a pivotal place in an all-time England eleven although wise selectors would want Hammond for his batting, Botham for his bowling and the two of them together in the slips.

As a young man, before physical bulk reduced the wonderful suppleness of his classical action, Botham was one of the most devastating genuinely fast bowlers of out- and in-swingers there has ever been. The first man to complete a Test double of more than 5,000 runs and 300 wickets, he was also a quite brilliant fielder, specialising at second slip where he would often stand closer than anyone else. He scored fourteen Test centuries and took five wickets in an innings on 27 different occasions, including his first Test match as a boisterous puppy of a cricketer in 1977.

That early zest left him after a sensational start in international cricket. His flamboyant enjoyment of the good things available to an international sporting celebrity – based on his father's advice that 'life is not a dress rehearsal, you know' – reduced his effectiveness, but he had phenomenal strength and stamina. They enabled him to remain a titan in what was, despite two more successful Ashes series in the 1980s, more often than not a struggling England side.

Cheshire-born but brought up in Somerset, Botham showed his promise as an MCC young cricketer at Lord's. Six foot two inches tall and soon to be a muscular fifteen stone, he was an eighteen-year-old boy, not yet the bull of a man he would become, when he first attracted wider notice with a courageous innings in a one-day quarter-final match for Somerset against the fire of the West Indies fast bowler Andy Roberts, then playing for Hampshire. The moment England picked him in 1977 he looked born to Test cricket. He made three centuries in his first seven games.

His springy and classical bowling action owed much to the advice of Tom Cartwright, the former Warwickshire and England all-rounder who was playing for Somerset when Botham joined the staff late in 1973. It had an easy rhythm about it, for all his brawn. His batting was based on sound principles that stood him in good stead when defence was necessary, but he hit the ball exceptionally hard.

He was by far the biggest English thorn in Australia's flesh from the start. In 1978-79 he took 23 wickets, held several brilliant catches and played outstanding attacking innings when England were in trouble in Sydney and Adelaide. In the series in Australia the following winter, arranged to mark the return of the World Series cricketers to their countries, he made 119 not out at Melbourne, took nineteen wickets in three Tests and then, in the one-off 'Jubilee' Test in Bombay, followed a century when England were in trouble with magnificently sustained swing bowling that earned him thirteen wickets in the match.

Making him England captain at 24 in 1980 meant testing him against the powerful West Indies both at home and away, and for a

time he was like Samson without his hair. He was still a match-winner in county cricket, scoring 228 against Gloucestershire, an innings that included ten sixes and 21 fours. He scored 182 between lunch and tea. But after making a pair in the Lord's Test against Australia the following season he resigned the captaincy. The return of Mike Brearley for the third Test at Headingley, when England were one down, galvanised him.

He took six for 95 in Australia's first innings of 401 and made 50 of England's paltry 174 in response. Following on, England were 105 for five against Dennis Lillee and Terry Alderman in their second innings when Botham came out to bat at seven, one place lower than his normal position. He chanced his arm and with glorious driving, cutting and hooking scored a century off 87 balls, going on to 149 not out with support from the tail. A chastened Australia were then bowled out for 111 by Bob Willis, who took eight for 43 to inspire an eighteen-run victory, only the second by a Test team following on.

At Edgbaston in the next match Botham settled the game with a final spell of five for eleven in 28 balls, as Australia again failed to chase a modest fourth-innings target. Then, at Old Trafford, still batting at seven, he made a thrilling 118 from 102 balls (100 from only 86), against high-class fast bowling in a dim light. The Ashes were back in English hands before his ten wickets in the sixth and final Test at the Oval.

His Old Trafford innings included six sixes, mainly from audacious hooks. Four seasons later, as Somerset captain, he hit no fewer than 80 in a season, a record. He was revered at Taunton and remained a national hero despite the fact that at the height of his fame he was, like Hammond before him, having his problems off the field, more publicly than those of his predecessor because of the changed nature of celebrity and the press. They included a period of suspension for being in possession of cannabis.

The loyalty of a model wife and the largeness of his own character, which is optimistic and generous, ensured that all was eventually well. 'Beefy' Botham remained a celebrity, undertaking a series of arduous walks that raised millions of pounds to help research into leukaemia, and often in the public eye as a television commentator. Into his fifties he was golfing, fishing and shooting, and still advertising a breakfast cereal that emphasised his image as a strong man. By now he possessed both a knighthood and a Bentley, both of which fitted his intense patriotism. Unlike some great players, he was a fulfilled man.

17. LEN HUTTON

Sir Leonard Hutton, b. 23 June 1916, Fulneck, Yorkshire; d. 6 September 1990, Kingston, Surrey

First-class: 40,140 runs (55.51), 173 wickets (29.51) and 400 catches
Tests (79): 6,971 runs (56.67), three wickets (77.33) and 57 catches

Brevity being the soul of wit, the distinguished playwright and passionate cricket aficionado Sir Harold Pinter put it very succinctly in his 1986 poem, *Hutton*:

I saw Hutton in his prime
Another time
another time.

I once remarked to John Woodcock, the cricket writer with the longest experience of all, that it was a pity that for all his greatness Len Hutton had to be such a dour player. But I had seen him only at the end of his career, when all the cares of English cricket had weighed heavily upon him. In his youth, Woodcock assured me, as Pinter surely would have done, he had been a joy to watch; the complete player and the true successor to Jack Hobbs as England's master batsman.

He was the second professional cricketer after Hobbs to be knighted for his services to cricket. The happy coincidence of

England's regaining the Ashes under his captaincy soon after the coronation of the Queen in 1953 had something to do with it, no doubt, but so did his record-breaking innings of 364 at the Oval against Australia in the flower of his youth in 1938, and the dignity of his bearing throughout his career. In Donald Trelford's book *Len Hutton Remembered* Jim Kilburn gave a thorough analysis of the character of the cricketer with whom he had travelled for 30 years. He was unfailingly and genuinely modest, utterly loyal to his wife Dorothy ('a damn sight better as Lady Dorothy than he was as Sir Leonard'), financially shrewd, glad to be playing cricket for a living, ambitious for the England captaincy but weighed down by the heavy responsibilities it entailed. They were, however, carried out with the same conscientiousness on and off the field.

Hutton was so good as a boy at his home club Pudsey that when he first came to the Yorkshire nets the coach, George Hirst, simply said that there was nothing that anyone could teach him. An operation on his nose in 1936-37 improved his frail health and for the next three seasons he was the best batsman in England. In 1937 he scored ten hundreds and 2,888 runs; in 1938, 1,874 runs at 60; with MCC in South Africa the following winter 1,168 at 64; and in 1939 another 2,883 at 62, with twelve hundreds.

He broke and dislocated his left arm in an accident in the gym during the war. After three bone grafts it was almost two inches shorter than his right arm and weaker, requiring changes to his technique. Ray Lindwall still thought him second only to Bradman: 'His judgement of length was so good … He didn't like bouncers but he didn't get out to them … He used to get away from the strike.'

No longer in his Pinteresque prime, perhaps, he remained the most reliable batsman in England, albeit not so dashing or carefree as Denis Compton. Mainly that was the result of having to prop up both Yorkshire and England. He was still capable of brilliance as well as implacable solidity. In the Sydney Test of 1946 he reeled off wonderful strokes to make 37 out of 49 in 27 minutes before his bat unluckily slipped in his hands. In June 1949 he suffered three ducks in succession but still scored 1,294 runs. In Australia in 1950-51 he averaged 88 in the five Tests, exactly 50 more than the next best England batsman, Reg Simpson, and 45 better than the top

Australian. Of his 129 centuries, nineteen were for England but only three of his wickets as an accurate leg-spinner came in Tests.

A pragmatic, cautious but also astute captain, he led England in 23 games and did not lose a rubber. He became an effective business-man, moving south to Surrey. His elder son, Richard, played for England and one of his grandsons, Ben, captained Middlesex.

16. KEITH MILLER

Keith Ross Miller, b. 28 November 1919, Melbourne; d. 11 October 2004, Melbourne

First-class: 14,183 runs (48.90), 497 wickets (22.30) and 136 catches
Tests (55): 2,958 runs (36.97), 170 wickets (22.97) and 38 catches

'If I had to choose one man to take a catch, take a wicket or hit a six to win the match, it would be Keith Ross Miller,' said John Arlott. 'The ladies loved him and every man wanted to be him,' said Michael Parkinson. 'There were many rumours about Keith and they were all true,' said Richie Benaud. 'He was a cavalier in a world of round-heads, a man of mood who could seize a game by the throat,' said John Warr.

A handsome man of generous nature who never took the game too seriously, he was probably the most charismatic cricketer there has ever been. He loved a crowd and played to it like the showman he naturally was. No one quite knew what to expect of him, except enter-tainment. He was as likely to follow one of his frequent bouncers with a slow leg-break as he was to bowl a yorker.

He was a natural athlete with a strong physique and a wonderful eye; a fast, incisive bowler with a vigorous body action, capable of sud-den inspirational bursts; a naturally aggressive, clean-hitting batsman;

and a brilliant fielder. He was not always a responsible cricketer, which mattered less in the powerful teams for whom he played after the Second World War than it might otherwise have done, but he could do almost anything on a cricket field when his mood was right.

The challenge of a big match excited him far more than one that was one-sided. It was typical, for example, that when the Australians scored 721 in a day against Essex at Leyton in 1948, Miller was quickly out for nought. But when Ray Lindwall and Alan Davidson were both injured before the Lord's Test in 1956, he took five wickets in each innings and Australia won. Despite a complete indifference to his own figures, they confirm that he was one of the greatest all-rounders.

He was only eighteen when he first played for Victoria in 1937-38, scoring 181 against Tasmania, despite hitting only five boundaries over the vast and no doubt thickly grassed outfield at the MCG. His Test career did not start until after a war in which, as a commissioned RAF officer, he had flown a Mosquito as a fighter pilot in hazardous raids over France and Germany. It explained both his carefree attitude to cricket and a serious side of his character that appreciated poetry and classical music.

Following his glorious 185 in 165 minutes for the Dominions eleven at Lord's in 1945 he made indelible marks in his first Test against England in 1946-47, bowling off-cutters on a sticky wicket at Brisbane to take seven for 60 after making 79. He scored a brilliant 141 at Adelaide, but bowling gradually became his stronger suit and he became forever bracketed with his new-ball partner, Ray Lindwall. Len Hutton found Miller the more difficult to play, not least because of his willingness to unleash bouncers.

A niggling knee injury made him less consistent, but he burst through England's top order at Melbourne in 1954-55 with an opening spell of three for five from nine overs. Against the West Indies later that season he scored 147 in the first innings of the first Test at Sabina Park, took over as captain in the field after Ian Johnson had injured a foot while batting and, as no great respecter of Johnson's captaincy, took pleasure in leading the side to a nine-wicket victory. In the fifth Test, also at Kingston, Australia won again, this time by an innings. Miller scored 109 and took eight for 167 in the match on the truest of pitches.

For the rest of his life Miller enjoyed himself, part of the time as a none-too-conscientious cricket writer. He travelled the world and never missed a summer in England, where his friends were legion and he was a frequent visitor to sporting events such as Wimbledon and Royal Ascot.

15. WILFRED RHODES

Wilfred Rhodes, b. 29 October 1877, Kirkheaton, Yorkshire; d. 8 July 1973, Branksome Park, Dorset

First-class: 39,802 runs (30.83), 4,187 wickets (16.71) and 764 catches
Tests (58): 2,325 runs (30.19), 127 wickets (26.96) and 60 catches

The figures produced by Wilfred Rhodes during his long, legendary career are simply staggering: over 4,000 wickets; almost 40,000 runs; more than 100 wickets in 23 seasons; more than 1,000 runs in 21; the double in sixteen. By sheer ageless craft he took more than 100 wickets at the age of 50.

First playing for Yorkshire in 1898, he took thirteen wickets for 48 in his second match against Somerset. Last playing for England at the age of 48 in 1926, he was the chief reason for the famous success at the Oval, when he took four for 44 in twenty overs in the second innings (and six for 79 in the match) to win back the Ashes.

A mere 22 years earlier he and his scarcely less legendary Yorkshire colleague, George Herbert Hirst (omitted herein only because some immortals had to be, and because his bowling was less effective in Tests), had shared the famous last-wicket stand that won another Oval Test against Australia. Hirst was in fact as much the winner of that game as its hero, Gilbert Jessop, but Rhodes at the time was still 'nobbut a lad' and he kept his head.

He started at number eleven for England and graduated by diligence, competence and common sense to the role as Jack Hobbs' opening partner. They put on 159 at Johannesburg in 1909-10 and 221 at Cape Town. Then, at Melbourne in 1911-12, they shared what is still England's first wicket record against Australia, 323.

Rhodes the batsman had grit, a very sound defence and a leaning cover drive. Rhodes the bowler was the greatest-ever exponent of flight. H.S. Altham left a perfect picture: 'An action of balanced economy but beautiful rhythm was the basis for supreme control of both length and direction; he could turn the ball on wickets that gave no help, and on those that did its bite and lift were deadly.' Add this to the profound character of the man, his patience, intelligence, shrewd analysis of the weaknesses of his adversaries and his refusal to wilt under pressure, and you have the explanation for his taking more wickets than any other player.

In his first season he finished with 154 wickets. In his second he bowled unchanged throughout the match against Essex at Leyton, taking fifteen for 56. After five seasons he already had 1,251 wickets, the haul of a full career for many a good bowler.

First picked by England in his second season, 1899, he should have been the match-winner for the first time in 1902 when he and Hirst bowled Australia out at Edgbaston for 36, Rhodes taking seven for seventeen, but the weather denied them. In 1903-04, on the first of his four tours of Australia, he took fifteen for 124 in the Melbourne Test and 31 at fifteen in the series – the prime reason, besides R.E. Foster's batting, for the fact that England went on to win the Ashes back following four consecutive defeats.

He went to South Africa twice and on England's first Test-playing tour to the West Indies in 1929-30 before he was employed as a coach by Harrow School. Hirst had already started work in the same role at Eton. Blindness forced Wilfred's retirement, but he accepted his decline with good grace. He would be taken to matches in his old age and sense with remarkable accuracy what was happening from the familiar sounds of bat on ball and, occasionally, the no less familiar tinkle of falling bails.

A Neville Cardus story of the wisdom of Rhodes in his playing days bears repetition. He and Yorkshire's steady in-swing bowler Emmott

Robinson went out after rain to inspect a sodden wicket. 'That'll be turning by four o'clock,' said Robinson. 'Nay Emmott,' was Wilfred's response, 'half past four.'

14. IMRAN KHAN

Imran Khan, b. 25 November 1952, Lahore

First-class: 17,771 runs (36.79), 1,287 wickets (22.32) and 117 catches
Tests (88): 3,807 runs (37.69), 362 wickets (22.81) and 28 catches
One-day internationals (175): 3,709 runs (33.41), 182 wickets (26.62) and 36 catches

Pakistan's greatest all-round cricketer was among the most gifted athletes ever to play the game, a man of moral courage and independent mind. An Adonis with an air of effortless superiority, he was adored by female admirers wherever he went and became the leader of his own political party, fighting corruption in high places. Imprisoned briefly by President Musharraf, the country's military leader, after objecting to the dismissal of independent judges, Imran was released as a hero but never captured a sufficiently large popular vote to hold office himself, partly, perhaps, because of the high-flying social life he had led during his years as a successful international cricketer. His marriage to a beautiful British wife of Jewish descent, Jemima Khan, née Goldsmith, was eventually dissolved.

Carrying himself on the field with a certain hauteur, he bowled at extreme pace after a long run and formidable leap, and specialised in very late inswing. He batted with an unmistakable air of class and made fielding look easy. When he really wanted to put on a performance, such as captaining his country in England or Australia or leading them to victory in the World Cup final, he generally did.

A cousin of two Test cricketers, Javed Burki and the equally gifted

Majid Khan, Imran was educated at Aitchison College in Lahore and later at Worcester Grammar School. He was the outstanding player of his generation at Oxford University, scoring a century in each innings against Nottinghamshire in the Parks in his year as captain, 1974. He played some cricket for Worcestershire from 1971 and was capped in 1976 when, against Lancashire, he scored 111 not out and took thirteen for 99 in the match.

Moving to Sussex the following year to be nearer London, he became part of a fearsome new-ball attack shared by the South African Garth Le Roux. Two one-day trophies were won by Sussex in Imran's time and the County Championship eluded them only narrowly in 1981, the year in which he subsequently admitted to roughing up one side of an old ball with a bottle-top to make it reverse swing (against the shine) during a match against Hampshire that had appeared moribund. In 1983 he made 1,260 runs in only half a season, and at Edgbaston, having top scored in both innings against Warwickshire, he came late into the attack because of an injury but proceeded to take six wickets for six in 23 balls, including a hat-trick. In 1983-84 he played for New South Wales, helping them to win the Sheffield Shield.

The first of his many inspiring performances in Test cricket came at Sydney in 1976-77 when his unremitting hostility earned him twelve wickets in the third Test, leading to Pakistan's first victory in Australia. Returning in 1981-82 he took sixteen wickets in three Tests at 19.5, a prelude to his fourteen for 116 against Sri Lanka at Lahore when he took eight for 58 in the first innings. He first captained Pakistan in England in 1982, averaging 53 with the bat and taking 21 wickets at 18.57 with the ball in a series that Pakistan deserved at least to draw.

He led Pakistan for most of the rest of his career in both Tests and one-day internationals, despite being sniped at by rival interests in Karachi and refusing to play in domestic cricket because he disapproved of its structure. In 1982-83, as the game's supreme all-rounder despite coinciding with the primes of Ian Botham, Kapil Dev and Richard Hadlee, he led his country to 3-0 series wins against both Australia and India, against whom he took 40 wickets in six Tests at a phenomenal 13.95 runs each. At Faisalabad he scored 117 and took eleven wickets in the match for the second successive time. His workload was such, however, that something had to give, and for almost three years he did not bowl in Test cricket because of a stress fracture in his left leg.

He returned, refreshed, to take 21 wickets as captain in England in 1987, including ten for 77 in the decisive victory at Headingley. Any thought of consolation for England at the Oval ended when Imran made a majestic 118. Away to the West Indies in 1987-88, he out-bowled the home fast bowlers – including Marshall, Walsh, Ambrose and Patterson – by taking 23 wickets at eighteen. Had it not been for what Imran claimed to be poor umpiring at Bridgetown, where the West Indies won by two wickets to level the three-match series, Pakistan would have inflicted upon the world champions their first home series defeat since 1973. But Imran enjoyed a final triumph by leading Pakistan to victory in the World Cup final of 1992 against England at Melbourne, dedicating it to his fundraising drive for a cancer hospital in Lahore in memory of his mother.

13. MUTTIAH MURALITHARAN

Muttiah Muralitharan, b. 17 April 1972, Kandy

First-class: 2,109 runs (11.15), 1,344 wickets (19.26) and 120 catches
Tests (127): 1,178 runs (11.32), 770 wickets (22.18) and 69 catches
One-day internationals (329): 610 runs (6.42), 505 wickets (22.74) and 127 catches

So full of zest did Muttiah Muralitharan appear when he took his 709th Test wicket to break the all-time record in his native Kandy in 2007, that no one would have betted confidently against his becoming the first man to take 1,000. For fifteen years the bright-eyed sorcerer from the Sri Lankan hills had been the most fascinating and talked-about bowler in the world.

An off-spinner who always got prodigious turn through the corkscrew twist of an extraordinarily supple wrist, he became the greatest match-winner of them all once he had practised, unveiled and perfected his 'doosra', a leg-break delivered over the back of his hand, cleverly disguised and spinning almost as far.

His skill is mesmeric, his action unique. Starting with a springy jog to the stumps from a slight angle, he transfers the ball with a vigorous tweak from his right to his rising left hand, as if spinning it up a shute, then restoring it to the bowling hand in time to arrive at the delivery stride nicely balanced to flick it out of his fingers, propelled by a vigorous upward motion of elbow and wrist.

There is so much more to Murali's success than his action. He has practised tirelessly to achieve almost impeccable control and his stamina and patience have been remarkable, not least in his own hot land. He bowled more than 6,300 overs before passing Shane Warne's record. Above all, his character – believing in himself and rebounding from the shock of being no-balled in Australia, not to mention various injuries – has withstood the inevitable setbacks.

At St Anthony's College in Kandy Murali was persuaded by his coach, Sunil Fernando, to give up fast bowling at the age of thirteen and to try off-spin. His rapid success soon attracted notice in Colombo, and careful nurturing in matches for Australia's A team led to a first Test cap against Australia in 1992. Six years later he produced perhaps his greatest performance overseas, taking sixteen wickets on the truest of Oval pitches in a one-off Test against England. He bowled 113 overs and five balls in the game, and had figures of 54.2-27-65-9 in the second innings.

Only his ordinary record against Australia has spoilt his record. In Australia it is twelve wickets at 75; against them, at home and away, 59 wickets at 36. To a large extent that is the result of controversy over his freakish action. Like his three brothers he was born with a slight bend in his arm, preventing him from fully straightening the right elbow. He was called for throwing there by two different umpires in Australia in 1995-96, but was eventually allowed to continue bowling by the ICC after detailed computer analysis of his action, which was filmed from 27 different angles.

For a time later in his career they forbade him, officially, to bowl his doosra but the ICC's cricket committee came to the conclusion that virtually all bowlers straighten their arm to some extent, and always have. Ultra slow motion film showed that Murali did so to less than 15 degrees, which has become the benchmark. Some respected judges think it was weak of the ICC to be so cooperative, but they knew that they would otherwise have been challenged in the law courts to the detriment of the game. More than that, they might have robbed cricket of one of its greatest entertainers.

Batsman after batsman has followed plans to combat and dominate him. The left-handers Graham Thorpe and Matthew Hayden were especially successful, but more often than not Murali had the last laugh. It was a hearty, infectious laugh at that. Throughout his international career, in Tests and 50-over games alike, his potency has enabled Sri Lanka to be a match for any team anywhere. He has been to Sri Lankan cricket what Don Bradman was to Australia's and W.G. Grace to England's.

His popularity, owing much to his fighting character and sunny temperament, was all the more remarkable for the fact that he is a Tamil, the eldest son of the manager of a biscuit and sweet manufacturer in Kandy. He is as much revered by the Sinhalese as by his own race, despite the long civil war between the extremist 'Tigers' of the north of the island, fighting for an independent state, and the Sri Lankan government.

12. GLENN McGRATH

Glenn David McGrath, b. 9 February 1970, Dubbo, New South Wales

First-class: 977 runs (7.75), 835 wickets (20.85) and catches
Tests (124): 641 runs (7.36), 563 wickets (21.64) and 38 catches
One-day internationals (249): 115 runs (3.96), 380 wickets (21.98) and
37 catches

Intense determination, a good cricket brain and the simplest of actions made Glenn McGrath, the gangly country boy from Narromine, one of the great fast bowlers of history, arguably the best of all. Almost from the moment that he joined forces with Shane Warne under the shrewd captaincy of Mark Taylor, Australia had the bowling resources to rule the cricket world.

Australia won 71 of the 103 Tests in which McGrath and Warne played together but, on figures, McGrath's influence was even greater. No fewer than 84 of his 124 Tests were won by Australia. It was only in the two Tests in which he was not fit to play that England won the matches in 2005 that enabled them, briefly, to regain the Ashes.

Very tall, and eventually also broad, strong and fit enough for prolonged hard work, with a back like a shield, he had an action that never varied and almost always looked rhythmical. A long straight run gave him momentum into a balanced delivery. His action has routinely been described as 'chest-on', but incorrectly so. His release of the ball came from an exceptionally high position after a full wheel of the body that started in the classical position, and his head remained level until well into his smooth follow-through. McGrath was the perfect example of accuracy being more important than sheer speed, especially since he was always fast enough (on average a little above 80 mph) to be genuinely hostile.

The ball invariably hit the seam close to the off stump, often lifted awkwardly and frequently either left the right-hander off the pitch or bit back sharply to go through the gate. The slope of the Lord's pitch, where he bowled magical spells from the Pavilion end in the Tests of 1997 (eight for 38) and 2005 (five for two in 31 balls) suited him perfectly.

He was, said Kerry O'Keeffe, the most unremarkable of remarkable bowlers. As Robert Craddock wrote in the 2008 *Wisden*: 'McGrath never had the pace of Brett Lee, the swing of Richard Hadlee, the intimidatory aura of a rampaging Dennis Lillee. Yet somehow he eclipsed them all – easily.'

He did not start playing until he was seventeen, but the former Test batsman Doug Walters spotted his coltish ability two years later when he played against Narromine and in the classic Australian way McGrath went to try his luck in Sydney, living for a time in a caravan.

A rapid improvement followed. He took five wickets in his first match for New South Wales, seven in the Shield final later that 1992-93 season, worked on his action at the Australian Cricket Academy and played his first Test in his eighth first-class match. Once established in the national team his accuracy, consistency and sheer professionalism were extraordinary.

It was McGrath who was the catalyst for Australia's first win in a series against the West Indies for twenty years. He gave them a taste of their own unpleasant medicine by bowling bouncers at them in the first Test at Bridgetown in 1994-95, taking eight wickets in the match, then had figures of six for 47 in the third Test to revive his team after they had been bowled out for 128.

For thirteen years in both Tests and one-day internationals he produced performances of this kind. He never played in a losing series at home, yet his average per wicket was even better (20.81) overseas than it was at home (22.43). On the subcontinent, where Dennis Lillee had failed (in Pakistan) and few fast bowlers have excelled, he took 72 wickets at 23, including ten in two Tests when Australia played Pakistan in temperatures reaching 51 degrees centigrade in Sharjah. His best Test analysis was eight for 24 against Pakistan at Perth in 2004-05. He had one long break after an ankle operation in 2005 and recovered fully.

Nowhere and nothing was too big a challenge. When he played fourteen first-class games for Worcestershire in 2000 he took 80 wickets at thirteen, and 114 wickets in all games. In the 45-over league both his strike rate of one wicket every 8.3 balls he bowled, and his economy rate, set new standards. He conceded an average of 2.16 runs an over, bettering a rate set by the famously parsimonious Derek Shackleton (over 40 overs) in 1969.

He was a steady fielder in the deep, slow by modern standards, and a determined but inept batsman who took more than three times as many one-day international wickets as he scored runs. A tyrant at times on the field, quick to ire and forever chuntering to himself when his bowling had fallen below his own exacting standards, he was a gentle soul off the field, with simple tastes. Soon after retiring he tragically lost his English wife following a long battle with cancer, leaving him with two young children.

11. MALCOLM MARSHALL

Malcolm Denzil Marshall, b. 18 April 1958, Bridgetown, Barbados;
d. 4 November 1999, Bridgetown

First-class: 11,004 runs (24.83), 1,651 wickets (19.10) and 145 catches
Tests (81): 1,810 runs (18.85), 376 wickets (20.94) and 25 catches
One-day internationals (136): 955 runs (14.92), 157 wickets (26.96) and
fifteen catches

A passionate cricketer who died sadly young, Malcolm Marshall took his 376 wickets at a cheaper cost than any fast bowler of the era of covered wickets, indeed cheaper than any truly fast bowler of the twentieth century. Sixty per cent of his Test victims were caught, more than a third of them by the wicket-keeper, and the majority of the others in the slips.

At a little under five feet eleven inches tall, and twelve stone, he was a slight figure by the standard of modern fast bowlers, but also lithe and whippy with a shimmering, quick-stepping sprint to the crease and a very fast arm. In his prime he combined electric speed with complete control that was intelligently and ruthlessly applied. He always had a plan for each opponent.

Obviously he benefited from the quality and pace of the three other fast bowlers with whom he generally operated during eleven years of intensive work for the West Indies but he outdid them all, and in domestic cricket for Barbados, Hampshire and Natal he never lost his competitiveness or dropped his standards. A sunny character when the day's combat was done, he was also useful for all of his teams as a stylish batsman and speedy fielder.

He had to compete for a regular Test place with the likes of Colin Croft, Wayne Daniel, Joel Garner, Michael Holding and Andy Roberts, and later with Patrick Patterson, Curtly Ambrose and Courtney Walsh. He was outstanding on the slow pitches of Pakistan

in 1980-81 but it was not until 1982, when he took 134 wickets at fifteen runs each, that he came to be regularly chosen by the Test selectors. He rapidly became the sharpest razor in the pack, taking 56 wickets in home and away series against India, 21 in a home series against Australia and 24 at eighteen in England in 1984. At Leeds he broke his left thumb in the field, but batted one-handed and then bowled in plaster to take seven for 53.

So his achievements mounted: away to Australia in 1984-85, 28 wickets at nineteen, including ten for 107 in the Adelaide Test; at home to New Zealand, 27 at eighteen in four Tests. Then, against an England batting team including Gooch, Gower, Gatting, Lamb and Botham – all of them fresh from a heady summer against Australia – he added 27 wickets at seventeen in 1985-86, having already reduced his opponents' morale by breaking Gatting's nose in a one-day international with one of the searing, skidding bouncers in which he specialised.

Having taken an incredible 35 wickets in five Tests in England in 1988 at only twelve runs each – deliberately slow pitches only accentuated his ability to move the ball about off the seam, not to mention swing it – he was disappointed to be left out of the West Indies side after 1991. He played another season for Hampshire and enjoyed an Indian summer for Natal, passing on his trade secrets to Shaun Pollock before becoming coach to a West Indies team that was now in decline.

10. ADAM GILCHRIST

Adam Gilchrist, b. 14 November 1971, Bellinger, New South Wales

First-class: 10,334 runs (44.16), 756 catches and 55 stumpings
Tests (96): 5,570 runs (47.61), 379 catches and 37 stumpings
One-day internationals (287): 9,619 runs (35.89), 417 catches and 55 stumpings

Before he found his feet by moving from his native New South Wales to play for Western Australia, Adam Gilchrist spent a summer in England, as young Aussies like to do. He pitched up one Friday evening at a club in the south east and asked if there was a game for a bloke who kept wicket a bit and sometimes opened the batting. The match-winning hundred that he scored the following day was laced with so many cleanly struck straight sixes that the game was over little more than an hour after tea. At every level thereafter, he batted with the same uninhibited confidence in his ability to dominate any attack.

Australia won each of Adam Gilchrist's first fifteen Test matches. He became the clean-hitting, clean-living symbol of his country's approach to cricket: virile, aggressive and uncompromising.

Perhaps the biggest single reason for Australia's run of almost unbroken success under Steve Waugh and Ricky Ponting, he averaged 47 in Tests at number seven and all the time batted like a left-handed Gilbert Jessop, either pressing home advantages or turning games his country's way with fearless, full-bladed hitting. For the first seven years of the twenty-first century, indeed, he was the game's greatest match-winner. A keen-eyed, agile wicket-keeper of high quality, he also took control of many a one-day international as a barnstorming opening batsman.

His striking rate in Test cricket was a record for anyone who scored in excess of 2,000 runs: 81.95 runs per 100 balls. In one-day internationals he improved that to 97. He retired from Test cricket with a record number of wicket-keeping dismissals. Thirty-seven of his 414 victims were stumpings yet, from only one more Test than Alan Knott, Gilchrist held 129 more catches. He was the only man to strike more than 100 sixes in Test cricket and scored the second-fastest century, off 57 balls against England in Perth in 2006-07.

In only his second Test in 1999-2000, having started with 81 off 88 balls in his first, he scored 149 not out to secure a very unlikely fourth-innings victory against a dumbfounded Pakistan attack in Hobart. At the Wanderers a little over two years later, South Africa's strong attack thought that Australia were going to be bowled out for a modest first-innings total at 293 for five. Gilchrist hijacked the match, scoring 204 not out. Australia declared at 652 for seven.

The bigger the occasion the more he tended to excel. In his first

World Cup final at Lord's he scored 54 off 36 balls; in his second in Johannesburg 57 off 48 balls and in his third at Bridgetown an extraordinary 149 from 104 balls, curiously with a squash ball under his left batting glove. Australia won all three games.

To his seventeen Test centuries he added sixteen in one-day internationals. What is more, he set a fine example in his approach to the game, walking when he got a touch that might not have been spotted in a World Cup semi-final in Port Elizabeth, and declaring to open up an Ashes Test at Headingley when he was Australia's acting captain.

9. SACHIN TENDULKAR

Sachin Ramesh Tendulkar, b. 24 April 1973, Bombay

First-class: 21,318 runs (58.56), 67 wickets (61.47) and 168 catches
Tests (156): 12,429 runs (54.27), 42 wickets (53.02) and 100 catches
One-day internationals (423): 16,460 runs (43.89), 154 wickets (44.19)
and 129 catches

Compact power, perfect timing, the ability to hit good balls for four, humility, discipline and extraordinary concentration have made Sachin Tendulkar the highest ever run-scorer in international cricket. It is doubtful whether any batsman in history has been quite so good so young as he was, or whether any great sportsman has conducted himself better despite a career spent constantly in the public eye.

As for Don Bradman, good footwork and profound mental strength have been more important than technique for Tendulkar. Only five foot five inches tall but very strong, his unusually heavy but perfectly balanced bats have been made for him in Sussex. He grips them hard, with his bottom (right) hand held unusually low on the handle, but plays many of his shots by instinct, steering the ball into gaps in the field by the late adjustment of supple wrists, and getting his power from a quick punch into the ball, like a boxer delivering the knockout blow.

His natural genius and capacity for hard work were evident as a schoolboy at Sharadashram Vidyamandir School in Bombay, where he was coached by Ramakant Achrekar. He scored a century for the school in the under-seventeen inter-schools Harris Shield competition when he was only twelve. Two seasons later his school-mate, the left-handed Vinod Kambli, shared his glory in a record partnership of 664 in a school match (Tendulkar scored 207 not out, 329 not out and 346 not out in successive games), but Kambli could not handle the fame and fortune that went with playing Test cricket for India.

Tendulkar was only fifteen when he made 100 not out in his first first-class match for Bombay. After making fifteen in his first Test innings, against Pakistan in November 1989, showing courage as well as his watertight technique, he scored 88 in his second match against New Zealand and compiled an astonishingly mature maiden Test hundred against England at Old Trafford in his fourteenth match, helping to save the game. He was seventeen years and 112 days old, not yet allowed by law to drive a car or sign his own tour contract, but quite old enough to save his country with a Test hundred.

Later on that tour he ran half the width of the outfield to hold an amazing catch in front of the sight-screen at the Nursery end at Lord's. On his first visit to Australia a year later he made centuries at Sydney and, on a fast and bouncy wicket, at Perth, where he was ninth out for 114. Inevitably there were times when he could not live up to extraordinary expectation in the years that followed, not least in high-profile one-day games, but once he started opening the batting in the 50-over matches he became remarkably consistent.

Only senior members of the British royal family would fully understand what life has been like for Tendulkar since he first played for India at the age of sixteen. The 'royals' are protected to an extent by protocol, but Tendulkar has had to learn for himself, never expecting to be treated differently from other international cricketers despite having been *primus inter pares* for at least fifteen years. Like Sunil

Gavaskar before him, he has been a demi-god; but whereas some mud stuck occasionally to his predecessor as India's most prolific batsman, no more than a grain of dust has sullied Sachin's reputation. He was accused of tampering with the ball against the laws in a Test in South Africa, but his one-match suspension was revoked.

Unlike those of royal blood he was not prepared for his fame, although a stable family background – his father was a professor of Marathi literature – helped him. He has traded the loss of free movement in India for the riches resulting from his success. He has to drive his Ferrari, or go to the temple, at night, and to live in a guarded compound to enjoy some private family life with his wife, who is a paediatrician, and two children. He must travel to big cosmo-politan cities, or to countries like the USA where cricket is a minority sport, if he wishes to be recognised only by a few rather than by every-one. He has been astutely advised in his business affairs, attracting multi-million-pound contracts for endorsements or to be associated with large companies.

True satisfaction has come only from success on the field, where each of his record number of Test hundreds has been celebrated with an ideal mixture of joy and modesty. Totally unspoilt by his success, he has maintained an extraordinary professionalism, not only in the way that he has conducted himself but in his complete dedication to his batting art. Before Australia's tour to India in 1998 he prepared for Shane Warne by getting spinners to pitch the ball into deliberately roughed-up turf outside his leg-stump, and in certain innings he would discipline himself not to play any stroke that he thought carried too much risk. He refused every invitation to cover-drive Warne throughout an innings of 241 not out at Sydney in 2003-04.

A less frequent match-winner than Brian Lara, his greatest con-temporary, he has been more a team man, apparently happier when not captaining India, and playing every innings according to the needs of the team and the situation of the match. He was also the first batsman to exceed 10,000 runs in one-day internationals. His fielding remained keen and lively, and he was still capable of useful spells of spin bowling that could include either leg-breaks or finger spin.

By the time that he surpassed Lara's aggregate, becoming the first batsman to go beyond 12,000 runs in his 152nd match, against Australia in October 2008, he was no longer able to dominate opposing attacks as he once had, having had an operation on his shoulder and chronic pain in his left elbow, but he remained the rock of India's batting. Two months later, against England in Madras, he used his vast experience to guide them to the fourth highest total ever scored to win a Test, 387 on a worn and turning pitch. With a champion's sense of theatre, but not an ounce of selfishness, the winning runs and his 41st Test century were simultaneous.

8. WALTER HAMMOND

Walter Hammond, b. 19 June 1903, Buckland, Dover, Kent; d. 1 July 1965, Durban, South Africa

First-class: 50,551 runs (56.10), 732 wickets (30.580), 819 catches and three stumpings
Tests (85): 7,249 runs (58.45), 83 wickets (37.80) and 110 catches

Wally Hammond in command at the crease was one of the most majestic sights that cricket has afforded: a galleon in full sail. You have only to see a photograph of his cover drive, or a film of his swift, muscular advance down the pitch to loft a bowler back over his head with a wonderful combination of power and poise, to know that he was one of the greatest batsmen of them all. Withal he was England's surest slip fielder and capable of devastating spells as a fast-medium bowler.

Such was his versatility that Raymond Robertson-Glasgow, who had to bowl sometimes to Hammond, placed him above Bradman and Constantine as the greatest cricketer of all between 1925 and 1935, when 'he would make a hundred or two against Australia, then bowl down their first three wickets, then make with ease a slip catch which others would not merely miss but not even have rated as a miss. But I count also the effect of his presence on a match alone; the influence on a bowler's feelings of the sight of Hammond taking guard at about 11.50 am, when lunch seemed far and the boundary near.'

He reached 1,000 runs before the end of May in 1927, commanding a Lancashire attack that included Ted McDonald by making 187 in three hours at Old Trafford. In the first innings of the same game, he had responded to the loss of Gloucestershire's first three wickets for eleven by striking 50 in 70 minutes and 99 in all. The following winter in Australia, when Bradman, the only man to eclipse him in his prime, played his first Tests, he scored 905 runs in the series at an average of 113. At Auckland in 1932-33, his 336 not out against New Zealand remained the highest Test score for five years. He made six other Test double hundreds. The regal 240 against Australia at Lord's in 1938 was the most memorable. He gave one half-chance to Bill O'Reilly in the covers, but the ball was travelling so fast that it split the fieldsman's fingers.

The burden of being England's best batsman between the prime of Hobbs and Sutcliffe and the establishment of Hutton and Compton weighed heavily at times, especially when he became captain after turning amateur in 1938, but his figures would have been still more extraordinary but for the Second World War. He finished top of the first-class batting averages in England in every season from 1933 to 1939.

His personal life, in the words of his biographer David Foot, was 'littered with mistakes, in business by listening to the wrong advice, in choosing at times unsuitable friends, in being seduced by fleeting avarice'. He married an unsuitable first wife, for her father's money, with unhappy outcomes for them both. Foot concluded that the venereal disease which he contracted in the Caribbean in 1927 largely accounted for his reputation for moodiness.

7. S.F. BARNES

Sydney Francis Barnes, b. 19 April 1873, Smethwick, Staffordshire; d. 26 December 1967, Chadsmoor, Staffordshire

First-class: 1,573 runs (12.78), 719 wickets (17.09) and 65 catches
Tests (27): 242 runs (8.06), 189 wickets (16.43) and twelve catches

A giant in every sense, Sydney Barnes of Staffordshire was to all batsmen like a judge to a convicted felon or a dentist looming over a patient who knows he has neglected his teeth for too long. He extracted 189 batsmen in 27 Tests and his contemporaries knew him simply as the greatest bowler of all.

A gaunt-faced man with wide eyes and an austere expression, he was tall, broad and straight-backed, with long arms and huge hands. The cricket ball was a weapon in his long, strong fingers and with them he could spin it, seam it or swerve it in the air at a mixture of paces, but a stock speed well above medium. Accounts suggest that he bowled with his middle finger over the seam (which was less pronounced then), with the first and third spread on either side. He had a bouncy run-up that culminated in even springier steps before a final leap, and a full circular swing of the arm that gave him a smooth, coordinated delivery without, Pelham Warner recorded, any significant bending of the back. Leg-breaks and off-breaks were whipped out of his hand at will.

Fiercely independent, he played most of his domestic cricket for his native county. For them, in 22 seasons, he took 1,432 wickets at a cost of eight runs each. In the North Staffordshire and three other northern leagues – the Lancashire, Central Lancashire and Bradford – he dominated more remarkably than any of the legion of Test cricketers of many nationalities who have since preferred the relatively easy workload of the weekend leagues, as opposed to daily first-class county cricket. In League cricket alone, Barnes took 3,741 wickets at an average of 6.68.

The proud professional simply knew his worth. He played a little for Warwickshire and Lancashire, but jealousy about the amount of money he earned in the leagues made him an ostracised figure in the Edgbaston dressing-room. He resolved to plough his own mighty furrow. In 1901 A.C. MacLaren, Lancashire's magisterial captain, had accepted the offer from Australia to take a touring team there the following winter, after a dispute with MCC. By August he had filled all but one place on the boat. He asked Barnes to play in Lancashire's last match, against Leicestershire and, having scored a century himself after a rain-interrupted first day, the captain declared at 328 for eight (Barnes had scored 32) before asking his guest to bowl the second over. His first ball, a fast leg-cutter, had one of the Leicestershire openers caught at slip and he proceeded to take six for 70 in 29 overs.

Within a fortnight Barnes had been offered £300 to tour Australia and Lancashire had offered £100 to his league club, Burnley, to buy him out of his contract. In the games leading to the first Test he took regular wickets, including twelve in the match with Victoria, but the opening Test in Sydney was only his ninth game of first-class cricket at the age of 28. He took nineteen wickets at seventeen in the first two Tests, one won, the other lost, but was over bowled in the second Test at Melbourne – six for 42 and seven for 121 in 64 eight-ball overs – and broke down with knee trouble early in the third.

Still hampered by knee pain in 1902, his resolution was widely questioned despite his taking 82 wickets at 21 for Lancashire. Bill Lockwood was preferred to him in the England team, and he played only one Test. Fully fit again by the following summer, he took 131 wickets at sixteen for Lancashire but, not happy with the terms offered for a renewal of his contract, he had a public row with the committee and returned to combine league cricket with his clerical job, using his copper-plate handwriting to copy and 'engross' legal documents.

His dispute with Lancashire caused a tremendous hullabaloo. 'Temperament in Barnes has always been deficient,' *Wisden* opined. 'He might have made a great name for himself, his natural gifts being so remarkable.'

He did not play for England again until 1907 when, ironically, the refusal by some other bowlers to agree to the terms offered for

the tour of Australia let him in again. He took 24 wickets in the Tests at 26 and bowled more than any other bowler on either side. Monty Noble of Australia described him unequivocally as the best bowler in the world. Yet when England returned to Australia in 1911-12 he had played only in nine of their last 32 Tests and most of his first-class appearances had been for the Players against the Gentlemen. After Australia's win in the first Test at Sydney – Barnes three for 107 and one for 72 – he finally proved his exalted status beyond doubt on a humid first morning at Melbourne. Despite signs of 'flu, he found vicious late swing and movement off the pitch in the opening spell of 9-6-3-4. This effectively won the match. Barnes finished the series with 34 wickets at 22 and the Ashes were regained.

He was 38 by now, but in the Triangular Test tournament against Australia and South Africa in 1912 he took 39 wickets at only ten runs each, and in South Africa in 1913-14 he proved as unplayable on matting wickets as he ever was on the often soft league pitches of the north. In four Tests, he took 49 wickets at ten apiece at the age of 40.

6. VIV RICHARDS

Isaac Vivian Alexander (Sir Vivian) Richards, b. 7 March 1952, St John's, Antigua

First-class: 36,212 runs (49.33), 223 wickets (45.15), 464 catches and one stumping
Tests (121): 8,540 runs (50.23), 32 wickets (61.37) and 122 catches

I first saw 'Vivi' Richards, as he was initially known on his home island, laying the England bowling to waste as a carefree young batsman playing for the Leeward Islands on England's tour of the West Indies early in 1974. It was thrilling. Soon he was playing for Somerset, scoring

192 not out in his second Test match at Delhi and running out three Australians in the World Cup final of 1975, each swift pick-up and lethal throw celebrated with leaps of uninhibited joy. By the time that he arrived in England a year later a sterner batsman had evolved, one who was to become easily the most commanding batsman of his generation.

A proud and passionate man with the physique of a heavyweight boxer, he had learned to discipline his super-abundant natural talent during the previous winter in Australia, when an innings of 175 against Western Australia had been followed by a run of modest scores in a Test series dominated by Australia's fast bowlers, Dennis Lillee and Jeff Thomson. Richards ended the series as an opening batsman, scoring 30, 101, 50 and 98 in the last two matches.

This was the start of an eight-month period in 1976 when he scored 1,710 runs in eleven Tests. Back at his favoured number three for a home series against India, he reeled off three imposing hundreds in the first three Tests. He maintained his form with batting of unrivalled majesty during the driest English summer in anyone's memory. He scored 232 in the first Test at Trent Bridge, 291 at a parched Oval in the last and 829 in the five matches at an average of 118.42.

His father, Malcolm, a warder at the prison that abuts the recreation ground in St John's, the folksy little capital of Antigua and Barbuda, was a fast bowler for the island who taught his three sons to be God-fearing. Despite the occasional show of temper in his youth Vivian, soon shortened by cricket writers to 'Viv', has always been a model of courtesy, with an engaging, burbling, slightly high-pitched laugh. Never very articulate, he earned universal respect both by the force of his batting and the dignity of his bearing.

From his youth he was locally well known for his rich gifts as a sportsman – he played World Cup football for Antigua – and he learned to channel the fires that burnt within. Soon developing a magnificent physique, with strong legs and broad shoulders tapering to a thin waist, he would saunter to the wicket like a gladiator entering the arena without a thought of failure, always wearing his maroon cap when playing for the West Indies even when others started using helmets. His command at the crease was instant. The faster his opponents bowled at him, the more fiercely he hooked and drove them.

There was a massive presence barring their way to the stumps, less because of any exceptional height or bulk about Richards than because he always looked to be in cool command, conveying, by the excellence of his technique and the apparent barn-door width of his bat, an effortless superiority. He never seemed to play the ball with anything other than the middle of his Duncan Fearnley or Slazenger blade and he always had time to get into position for the shot he had chosen. The moment when he walked across his stumps to lift Mike Hendrick's last ball of the West Indies innings high into the Mound stand at Lord's in the 1979 World Cup final hangs in the memory. He made 138 in that innings and scored another century in the Gillette Cup final for Somerset later in the season.

Neither of these innings was the best of his naturally prolific career in one-day cricket. Early in 1985, on a cold day at Manchester, he found himself batting with the tail after the West Indies had been reduced to 102 for seven. The ninth wicket fell at 161. He scored 189 not out from an eventual total of 272, hitting five sixes and 21 fours. Earlier in the year he had taken over the captaincy of the West Indies from Clive Lloyd. He handled his responsibility with visible pride, often tested and criticised, smiling less than before perhaps, but determined to maintain their supremacy over everyone else. He never lost a series under his command.

Because of Richards, and the fast-bowling prowess of his country-man Andy Roberts, a Test match was awarded to Antigua for the first time in 1981, against England. He marked the occasion with his four-teenth Test hundred. Ten more followed including, on the same St John's recreation ground, a staggering domination of a reputable England attack led by his ageing friend Ian Botham in April 1986. Striking seven sixes, he reached his hundred from 56 balls, the fastest ever. It set up a declaration in the second innings, after which England were defeated for the tenth time in Richards' first ten Tests against them as captain.

He played some cricket for Glamorgan late in his career, helping them to a Sunday League title, and for Queensland in 1976-77, as well as in World Series Cricket. He finished with 114 first-class hundreds. He bowled off-breaks, often very effectively, and remained a superb fielder.

5. JACK HOBBS

Sir John Berry Hobbs, b. 16 December 1882, Cambridge; d. 21 December 1963

First-class: 61,237 runs (50.65), 108 wickets (24.89) and 332 catches
Tests (61): 5,410 runs (56.94) one wicket (165.00) and seventeen catches

No bad word was ever published or, apparently, spoken about a batsman who wearied bowlers for 30 years by the unrivalled mastery of his batting. It marks Sir John Berry Hobbs as little less than a saint, as well as a popular hero. He was in every way the model of cricket's art and spirit.

Archie MacLaren wrote a book about him simply entitled *The Perfect Batsman* and John Arlott, having described in prose the 'steady grey eyes set in a network of wrinkles engraved by sunshine and laughter', also encapsulated his mastery in verse:

There was a wisdom so informed your bat
To understanding of the bowler's trade
That each resource of strength or skill he used
Seemed but the context of the stroke you played.

In a career that started for Surrey in 1905 and ended in 1934, Hobbs was the unruffled master of his craft, repeatedly succeeding against both the fiercest fast bowling and the most venomous spin, not least on the 'sticky' pitches that, drying out after rain, brought out his genius. At the Oval in 1926 and at Melbourne in 1928-29, he and Herbert Sutcliffe overcame balls spitting at them from a length to inspire unlikely Test victories with famous opening partnerships of 172 and 105.

Hobbs was a Cambridge man inspired by Tom Hayward, who had followed the example of his father and grandfather in playing for

Surrey, scored 104 first-class hundreds and paved the path for Hobbs to the Oval before becoming his first opening partner. Young Jack, the eldest of twelve children whose father, John, was first a net bowler at the University ground, Fenner's, then groundsman at Jesus College, played wherever he could, but it was only through Hayward that he was able to get a trial at the Oval. By the time that he had qualified for Surrey by virtue of residence he was already an accomplished batsman, swift to spot the ball and to get into position to play it with unhurried elegance.

He scored 88 in his first match against a Gentlemen of England XI captained by W.G. Grace, and two weeks later made 155 against Essex in his first Championship match, winning his county cap instantly.

Every challenge that followed was tackled with skill, dignity and, usually, success. He augmented his runs by his brilliance in the field, especially at cover point from which position he would lure batsmen into risking a quick single by his apparent lethargy, then swoop. He ran out no fewer than fifteen batsmen on MCC's tour of Australia in 1911-12. By the same speed and anticipation, he was himself a brilliant judge of a run. He could even bowl effectively at times, swinging the ball away from right-handers with an easy action. He opened the bowling three times in Test matches in South Africa in 1909-10, taking his only Test wicket there.

On that tour he also countered the considerable threat of South Africa's googly bowlers, notably Vogler and Faulkner, top scoring three times out of four as the two wrist spinners took 35 of England's 40 wickets in the first two Tests, both home wins, and 187, the first of his fifteen Test hundreds, at Cape Town. Hobbs averaged 67, far ahead of any other England player in a lost series. Two winters later in Australia he scored centuries in three successive games, all won by England. There were to be six more hundreds against Australia, whose opposition was invariably the acid test.

Frank Woolley said of Hobbs: 'Only those who saw Jack before 1914 knew him at his very best.' But the flair of his early play was tempered by experience after a war spent first in a munitions factory, then with the Royal Flying Corps. From 1914 to the season before his retirement (1933) he scored 35,017 runs, averaging below 51 only once at home or on tour, and better than 60 eight times. He scored

131 centuries in those fifteen years, 98 of them after the age of 40. In 1925, at the age of 42, he scored ten hundreds in his first twelve games of the season.

No-one has ever scored more runs in first-class cricket than Hobbs. In all he shared 166 opening partnerships of more than 100, including fifteen with Herbert Sutcliffe and eight with Wilfred Rhodes for England, and 63 for Surrey with Hayward's successor, Andy Sandham, who recalled to me in his old age that among his senior partner's virtues had been an ability to count to six. It was a hint that, like all hungry batsmen, Hobbs liked to keep the strike when he was on top. Yet there was complete truth in his reflection: 'Centuries never bothered me, nor records really, nor averages. Of course I was earning my living but it was batting I enjoyed. I can say I always did enjoy it until, at the end, my legs got tired.'

Often described as looking frail, he actually had large thighs and forearms but the lightness of his footwork concealed his strength. Only a very fit man could have lasted so long. Money from his first benefit from Surrey in 1919 was invested in his sports shop in Fleet Street, and later in his four children.

4. SHANE WARNE

Shane Keith Warne, b. 13 September 1969, Melbourne

First-class: 6,919 runs (19.43), 1,319 wickets (26.11) and 264 catches
Tests (145): 3,154 runs (17.32), 708 wickets (25.41) and 125 catches
One-day internationals (193): 1,016 runs (13.02), 291 wickets (25.82) and 80 catches

Shane Warne carried the banner for leg-spin bowling into the twenty-first century with trumpets blasting. Until his arrival in Australia's team in 1993 it had lain hidden towards the bottom of a cupboard in the dressing-room, tattered, faded and almost forgotten.

His greatness lay not just in his tremendous skill and possibly unequalled accuracy as a wrist spinner, but also in his charisma. He conveyed to opponents and spectators alike the impression not only that he was thoroughly enjoying every match he played, but also that he was confident that his team would win. Australia, in fact, won 92 of the 145 Tests in which he played. No one in any Test team has been on the winning side so often and that, of course, was no coincidence.

Above all his achievements was his demolition of the widespread opinion that, in an age of heavy bats, increasingly muscular, more aggressive batsmen and shorter boundaries, the tempting beguilements of the slow bowler were a luxury that could not be afforded in the higher reaches of the game.

With his freakish action, Muttiah Muralitharan, who was increasingly Warne's unspoken rival, has taken more wickets; but he did not change the game to the extent that the Australian did by restoring wrist spin to international cricket, and therefore to the consciousness of young players everywhere. He made something of a point when in 2003 he took 26 wickets at only twenty runs each in Sri Lanka to beat his 'challenger' to 500. (Murali actually took 28 at 23, but Australia won all three Tests.) Warne retired with the record, 708 from 145 Tests between 1991 and 2007. Despite the need for major operations on his bowling hand and his right shoulder, he had by then bowled more overs in Test cricket than anyone.

Comfortably the most influential Australian cricketer since Don Bradman, he experienced notoriety as well as adulation and fame. He could not resist some of the temptations of life as an international sportsman, especially when he was away from home. 'Sometimes I feel as though I am playing a part in a soap opera,' he once said, and in 2008 the Australian production *Shane Warne – The Musical* did not eschew the seamier side of the great spinner's life. They included his suspension for taking a drug banned to sportsmen in a bid to get himself fit for the 2003 World Cup after the operation on his shoulder, and a fine for accepting money from an Indian gambler to replace money he had lost in a casino. Later, he felt obliged to give his bene-factor what he deemed to be unimportant information about such things as weather and pitch conditions. He always enjoyed a gamble, and when he retired from first-class cricket he became a part-time professional poker player.

His mistakes cost him his marriage but not the affection of the great majority of those who watched and played with him. They also barred his way to the captaincy of Australia, for which first Steve Waugh, then Ricky Ponting, were preferred. His skill as a captain of Victoria, of Hampshire (in 2000 and from 2004 to 2007) and the 'Rajasthan Royals', first winners of the Indian Premier League, proved him to be a most enterprising leader with a sensitivity to those with whom he was playing. The more his fame and success grew, the more he tended to push gamesmanship to the limit in talking to umpires and opposing batsmen.

He had such charm that he generally got away with it. In any case, his lustre as a cricketer is ineradicable. Starting his brief, measured approach to the crease with a few walking strides, he mixed occasional googlies, top spinners and the under-spinner, or flipper, with stock leg-breaks that would turn more or less according to his plan. He was uncannily accurate – there was practically never a long-hop or full-toss to relieve the pressure that he built around batsmen – and he was also as cunning as any of the great spin bowlers. After his shoulder operation he got many wickets with LBWs – and should probably have had many more – as batsmen tried to sweep him or misread the ball going straight on.

His trademark in his prime, between 1993 and 1998, was the prodigiously big leg-break, bowled with a vigorous twist of the shoulder and from strong fingers. Often, most famously with the ball that bowled Mike Gatting at Old Trafford in 1993, his first in an Ashes Test, sharp turn would be preceded by an inward dip of the ball towards the right-hander's toes, opening up his defence to make the break that followed even more lethal. Left-handers were no more immune. At Sydney in 1996 the West Indian Shivnarine Chanderpaul was playing brilliantly when he drew back to cut a ball that had pitched two feet outside his off-stump. It not only bowled him but actually hit his leg-stump. At Edgbaston in 2005 Warne bowled Andrew Strauss with a similar ball that the batsman had deemed quite safe to leave.

In that 2005 series he was heroic in defeat. He took 40 wickets at nineteen, sixteen more than anyone else on either side. Much more often he was a winner who thrived on finishing Test matches by bowling opposing teams out in the last innings of a match. His second Test captain, Mark Taylor, told Warne's biographer, Simon Wilde: 'Normally, if we gave Warney enough runs on the board on the last day it would be all over by about 5 pm.' Whenever the opposition had to make substantial runs in the fourth innings, Australia were favourites. At home, they never lost in such circumstances when Warne was in the team.

He took more than five wickets in an innings 69 times and, to his even greater pride, perhaps, he scored two first-class centuries, coming agonisingly close to a Test hundred too, making 99 against New Zealand at Perth in 2001-02 and 90 against England at Old Trafford in 2005, a typically bold and defiant effort that kept his side in the match. By talent and practice he became an outstanding close catcher, taking over at first slip from Mark Taylor.

3. GARY SOBERS

Sir Garfield St Aubrun Sobers, b. 28 July 1936, Bridgetown, Barbados

First-class: 28,315 runs (54.87), 1,043 wickets (27.74) and 407 catches
Tests (93): 8,032 runs (57.78), 235 wickets (34.03) and 109 catches

No cricketer has so often and so easily reached sublime heights as batsman, bowler and fielder as Garfield St Aubrun Sobers, a lithe Barbadian of consistently sunny temperament who found cricket as easy as walking. His very walk, indeed, was distinctive, a loping movement all his own that spelt trouble for opponents whenever he took the ball or emerged from a pavilion to bat.

Left-handed as both batsman and bowler, his versatility was unique. He batted with peerless stylishness, usually without a cap, fielded like a cat anywhere but with special brilliance close to the wicket on the leg-side to Lance Gibbs's off-breaks and was, famously, three bowlers in one.

He could, and often did, take the new ball, bowling fast left-arm and either bouncing the ball across the wicket or swinging it effort-lessly late into the right-handers. He had a beautiful sideways-on action with a long-striding but easy run-up followed by a full sweep of the bowling arm. He could also bowl chinamen and googlies or, more often, left-arm orthodox, the skill that first got him into the West Indies team. As a batsman alone he was one of the greatest there has been, with a huge backlift that seemed always to allow him to get on top of even the highest-bouncing balls. In defence he was watchful, straight from the textbook, but when he attacked he would swing his Slazenger bat 360 degrees with thrilling élan.

In any one of these disciplines he could have been a world-beater had he concentrated solely on each. Combining all of them and applying them to whatever the occasion of the conditions of pitch and weather demanded, he was potentially a match-winner in every game that he played. There was about him that air of supreme natu-ral talent that has only been equalled in any sport since by the golfer Tiger Woods. Sobers never had the same dedication as the American. Had he done so he might never have finished on a losing side, but he enjoyed himself, and entertained, much more. With Sobers, a buck-toothed smile was never far away.

He was the son of a merchant seaman who was drowned after his ship was sunk in 1942. He was born with five fingers on each hand, the extra two being removed in his boyhood. He played soccer, golf and basketball for Barbados and first appeared for the island as a cricketer at the age of sixteen, against the Indian touring team. At sev-enteen he was a Test cricketer, and in 1958 against Pakistan at Kingston he became world famous by scoring 365 not out to break Len Hutton's world Test record. He scored 824 runs at 137 in that series. He was only 21.

A year later he was driving in the car accident in England in which his friend and West Indian teammate, the Jamaican Collie Smith, was killed. He resolved to make the most of his own survival, drinking and partying hard for the rest of his career while playing cricket all round the world, including for Nottinghamshire and South Australia. He was the only man to have scored the Australian domestic double of 1,000 runs and 50 wickets – he did it twice – and in 1968 he struck six sixes in a six ball over against Glamorgan at Swansea, a feat captured by a television cameraman, happily for everyone except perhaps the bowler, Malcolm Nash.

His energy was astonishing. He played in every Test for the West Indies from 1955 to 1972. Against India in 1958-59 he made 557 runs at 92, and against England in 1959-60 greeted an attack led by Fred Trueman and Brian Statham by scoring 154 for Barbados. He followed up by making 226 in the first Test and 709 in the series at an average of 101, sharing a partnership of 399 with Frank Worrell. Having humbled England's best bowlers, he did the same in Australia the following winter, scoring 251 for South Australia against a New South Wales attack containing Alan Davidson and Richie Benaud.

Captaincy, a lavish night life and the need – and desire – to do so much bowling eventually took some of the edge off his batting, quite apart from the fact that he started to go in a little lower in the order – generally at six – to balance the sides he played for. In England as captain in the 1966 series he scored 722 runs at 103 and took twenty wickets at 27.25. He saved his team in the Lord's Test by adding 274 with his cousin, David Holford, and at Headingley, in the game that settled the rubber, he scored 174 and took eight for 80 in the match. In thirteen of his 22 Test series he took at least ten wickets, and 26 of his 86 centuries were scored in official Test matches.

He enjoyed himself too much off the field, perhaps, to be especially outstanding for much of the time when captaining the Rest of the World in Australia in 1971-72, a series that replaced the visit by South Africa that had originally been scheduled. Yet Sir Donald Bradman described his innings in the New Year 'Test' at Melbourne as being 'probably the best ever seen in Australia, one of the historic events of cricket'. He scored 254 in six hours, sixteen minutes with two sixes and 35 fours against an attack led by the rapidly flowering fast bowling of Dennis Lillee.

Racing and golf were his chief recreations in retirement. He gave too much away to the bookies but his bank balance was restored when he won a large prize in the Barbados national lottery. Such was the esteem and affection in which he was held that it was believed by those in the know to have been more than a happy coincidence.

2. W.G. GRACE

Dr William Gilbert Grace, b. 18 July 1848, Downend, Bristol; d. 23 October 1915, Mottingham, Kent

First-class: 54,211 runs (39.45), 2,808 wickets (18.15) and 875 catches
Tests (22): 1,098 runs (32.29), nine wickets (26.22) and 39 catches

Whether W.G. was the greatest cricketer ever to buckle a pair of pads I have taken impertinent leave to doubt. That he was the most famous there has ever been is not, of course, in question. He remains the embodiment of cricket. His life gives a snapshot of middle-class England in the era of its greatest importance in the world.

Cricket only became, officially, a legal pastime in 1845, along with other ball games, although the ancient law against them had long lain unenforced. Three years later William Gilbert was the fourth son to be born to Martha, wife of the cricket-loving Henry Mills Grace, a doctor who had moved from Somerset to Downend on the outskirts of Bristol. W.G. had the good fortune to be brought up as middle-class England was embracing cricket with fervour.

A practice area on the site of a flattened orchard gave the Grace family room to practice together under the supervision of Gilbert's mother's brother, Alfred Pocock. In 1854, as the Crimean war was about to begin, the six-year-old Gilbert watched his father and maternal uncle playing together for West Gloucestershire against the touring All England XI. At the age of fifteen Gilbert himself, 'full of life and vim', played against All England himself for Bristol and District, scoring 32 and 22. A season later, now over six foot tall, broadening out fast and loose-limbed, he scored his first century, for South Wales CC against the Gentlemen of Sussex on the old ground at Brighton. Soon he was the talk of a game that was fast being opened up by the spread of the railways.

By the end of his career it had captured the imagination of the urban as well as the rural working class too, to a large extent as a result of his own exploits. At Trent Bridge in 1871 the *Sporting Life* recorded that he had to 'pass to his dressing-room through a living lane of excited hand-clapping people, who had, directly the last wicket fell, rushed to the pavilion enclosure like a swarm of bees to applaud and stare at the Gloucestershire gentleman'. Of course, there was no television then. It was the only way to see him and the great beard, black in his youth, gradually going grey, made the doctor unmistakable.

Precious black and white film of Grace, batting in the nets late in his august career, shows just a glimpse of the supreme sporting champion of the age. He played the ball late, like all great batsmen, but he hit it also off both the front and back foot and on both sides of the wicket. Style had mattered more in the past but his pragmatism as well as his skill set him far apart from the rest. His mastery of all bowlers, not least the quick ones and even on rough pitches, made him popularly 'The Champion'.

As a young man he was also a champion runner and hurdler. Naturally outstanding in the field, he was a very effective round-arm medium-paced bowler. Later, as his bulk grew, he turned to spin and guile.

When he was eighteen, in July 1866, he scored 224 not out for England against Surrey at the Oval, and 173 not out for Gentlemen of the South against Players of the South. Two years later he made his first century for the Gentlemen against the Players. The 'Gents' had lost their last nineteen games in this fixture when first Grace played for them. When he last played in it in 1906, they had lost only four more times.

He was at his supreme best in his twenties, before qualifying as a

medical doctor in 1879. In 1871 he became the first man to score 2,000 runs in a first-class season, averaging 78, then a phenomenal performance despite improving pitches. In 1873 he became the first to score more than 2,000 runs and also to take 100 wickets, a feat that he repeated every season until 1878 and twice in the 1880s.

In 1876 he scored 400 not out in a minor match against 22 of Grimsby for the United South of England XI, seeing no need to interrupt his innings despite the birth of his second son, Henry, on the second of the three days of the game. If that was a case of bullying weak opposition (albeit 22 of them), his 2,622 runs in first-class games that season were scored at an average of 62. In hot weather in August, playing for Gentlemen of MCC against Kent at Canterbury, he responded to a first innings deficit of 329 by scoring 344, beating the record for first-class cricket that had stood for 56 years. Two days later he played for Gloucestershire against Nottinghamshire at Clifton, scored 177, then took eight for 69 in the second Nottinghamshire innings to inspire a ten-wicket victory. A day later, this time at Cheltenham, Gloucestershire took on Yorkshire and W.G. scored 318 not out in a total of 528. He scored more runs in August than any other man had ever scored in a complete season.

This was the apogee but in 1895, at the age of 46, he became the first batsman to score 1,000 runs in May and the first to reach 100 first-class hundreds. There was less startling success for him in the early days of international cricket, but he went on two tours to Australia and scored the first century in an official Test in England, 152 at the Oval in 1882.

He and his brothers (E.M. and G.F. also played Test cricket) were the driving forces in the formation of Gloucestershire CCC and, from 1871 until he resigned after a dispute with the committee, W.G. was the captain. He formed London County and played for them from 1900-04. Having retired because 'the ground was getting too far away' he took up golf, curling and bowls, captaining England in the first-ever bowls international, against Scotland in 1903.

Grace was no saint, sometimes pushing gamesmanship to the limit, but for the last 30 years of the nineteenth century he had been the country's greatest batsman and most famous sportsman. Thanks partly to his beard, his ruddy countenance vied with Queen Victoria's and W.E. Gladstone's as the most recognisable face in England. He made plenty of money from cricket – he was, for long periods, to all intents and purposes a professional – but these days the agents and image-makers would have multiplied his wealth many times.

1. DON BRADMAN

Sir Donald George Bradman, b. 27 August 1908, Cootamundra, New South Wales; d. 25 February 2001, Adelaide, South Australia

First-class: 28,067 runs (95.14), 36 wickets (37.97), 131 catches and one stumping
Tests: 52, 6,996 runs (99.94), two wickets (36.00) and 32 catches

From the late 1920s until his retirement in 1949, the greatest of all specialist batsmen had a wider role as a hero of popular culture and the unwitting symbol and unifier of the Australian nation. Don Bradman's unequalled batting achievements, and the fact that he was playing at a time when his country was asserting its right to complete independence, made him the most famous cricketer since W.G. Grace. Like the Champion himself his steely determination, hunger for success and genius for sport put him in a different class from any contemporary. By a whisker, if that is the appropriate phrase, he may be deemed the greatest of all cricketers, because his superiority over all contemporaries was even greater.

He was brought up in the country town of Bowral in New South Wales, where he taught himself to bat by hitting a golf ball rebounding from the brick stand of a water tank in his parents' back yard. When he came to England as a 21-year-old in 1930, he had already scored the highest Australian first-class score of 452 not out for New South Wales against Queensland. He scored a century in the first Test,

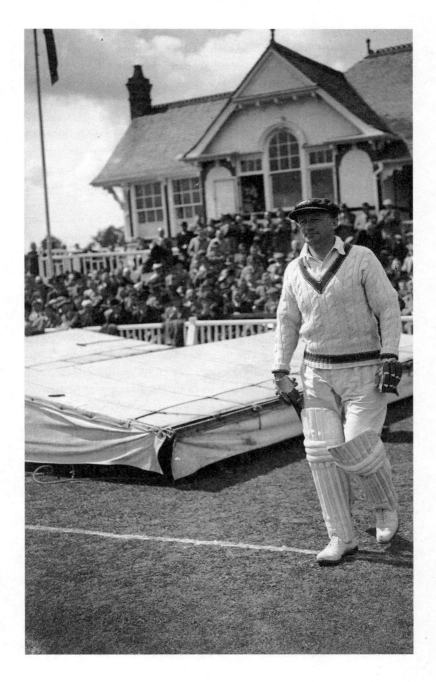

a double century in the second, 334 in the third at Leeds (then the world record Test score) and another double century in the fifth at the Oval. At Headingley he had scored a hundred before lunch, another in the middle session, and a third between tea and the close.

Against the South African touring team in 1931-32 he was still more merciless, scoring 1,190 runs against them in eight innings, three for New South Wales, at an average of 170. In five Test innings his average was 201.5. Such brilliance and remorselessness spawned Douglas Jardine's ruthless strategy in the return series in Australia, the cricketing equivalent of the Royal Navy's determination to sink the German battleship *Bismarck* in 1941.

Bradman was merely scathed by bodyline bowling but his batting average of 56.57 in 1932-33, fourteen runs higher than anyone else's, represented failure, embarrassment and defeat for him. Had he not been so cut down to size in that series, his final Test average would have been more than 100. Famously, it was 99.94, and in first-class cricket he scored 117 centuries, on average a hundred every third time that he batted.

He continued to dominate through the 1930s, to some extent a man apart in the dressing-room because of his single-mindedness and his controversial move to Adelaide to accept a lucrative job as a stock-broker in 1934. At the end of his tour of England that year he had an emergency operation to remove an acutely inflamed appendix, and only narrowly avoided the peritonitis that might have been fatal. This was a front-page drama, with his young wife Jessie summoned to travel by sea from Australia. He had a long convalescence but in 1936-37, inevitably, became Australia's captain.

When G.O. Allen's England side arrived at Freemantle they were greeted with the news that the new leader's last seven first-class innings had been 233, 357, 31, 0, 1, 369 and 212. Australia came back from defeat in the first two Tests to win the series 3-2. Bradman had innings of 270, 212 and 169 in the three games that transformed the series. Used as a PT instructor early in the war, he was invalided out of the army in 1941 but returned to cricket afterwards almost by popular demand. He captained his unbeaten team to England in 1948 with pragmatism, and made a great diplomatic success of his final visit.

Such were his reactions, fitness, keenness, intelligence and deep determination that he would have been a champion in any era since, not least the present one. It is true that the need to change tempo for 50, and now for 20-over, cricket against defensive fields and often on slower pitches would have tested even so fast a scorer as the Don, but in his prime he would have relished and risen above the challenge. His speed of foot and eye, not to mention modern bats, would have enabled him to compensate for a slight physique compared to some of the muscular players of today. His preference for keeping the ball along the ground would either have been tempered by a calculated decision to hit some balls for six – no batsman ever played the percentages so shrewdly as Bradman – or by his skill in finding gaps in the field with full-blooded strokes played late.

Short-pitched bowling would have been no handicap given the extra protection of a helmet. His powers of concentration – he scored 37 double and twelve triple centuries – would have ensured the same prolific achievements in first-class cricket now as then, especially given covered pitches. That he could not bat on wet or sticky pitches was a myth based largely on a couple of failures against Hedley Verity on the drying pitch at Lord's in 1934. R.C. Robertson-Glasgow, viewing him as both bowler and critic, dismissed the idea. 'He was,' he wrote, 'that rarest of nature's creations, an artist without the handicap of an artistic temperament.'

There was another paradox: he was a hero with the masses but not a popular man with most of his team-mates and opponents. He was too private and single-minded for that. Bill O'Reilly, his rival from boyhood, said: 'He felt it his bounden duty to reduce every bowler to incompetency.'

The academics Tony Shillinglaw and Brian Hale have analysed his 'continuous rotary batting process', the bat starting its backlift over second slip as with many great batsmen, looping down straight into the ball and following through in a second loop. They became convinced that it was the method that explained the phenomenon. But there was obviously more to it than technique, or even natural skill. It was his iron will and concentration that set him apart.

They must have made him equally successful at tennis – a game he toyed with successfully as a boy – or golf, which he played after retiring, getting down to scratch. He never bowled seriously but was one of Australia's finest cover fielders. His intelligence and fame ensured a prosperous career as a stockbroker but he gave back a great deal to cricket as an administrator, selector and copious letter-writer.

CONCLUSION

Edith Piaf had no regrets, Frank Sinatra a few. I'm afraid I have plenty. After reading my selections again it is not so much those chosen as those who had to be left out who embarrass me. There can be no looking back and I would not apologise for a single one of the men who made it into the top 100. It does not stop one wondering, however, about those whose omissions amount to the greatest injustices.

Clem Hill, Dudley Nourse, Jock Cameron, Martin Crowe, Jeff Dujon, Inzamam-ul-Haq, Alec Stewart, Anil Kumble, Younis Khan, Ramnaresh Sarwan, Mike Procter, Matthew Hayden, Mohammad Azharuddin, Saqlain Mushtaq, Derek Underwood, Andy Roberts, Joel Garner, Jeff Thomson, Bobby Simpson or Virender Sehwag? I could name three teams in batting order, and still feel afterwards like the Yorkshire sages in a pub who, having chosen eleven Yorkshiremen for their all-time England eleven, realised that they had left out W.G. Grace. 'Yes,' said one to the others as they contemplated the heresy: 'But who could we have left out?'

I prefer to dwell on those players who might be included in any volume similar to this one published ten or more years hence. In particular one wonders to what extent their fame will be built upon exploits in the one-day, rather than the Test, arena. Inexorably, it seems, Test cricket, on which supreme form of the game all the foregoing judgements have been made, is losing ground to Twenty20, the Keystone Cop form of the game that has undeniable attraction but that, as anyone who has played cricket to any decent level knows, is as superficial as it is snazzy.

There is no denying that, outside England, Test cricket currently attracts smaller crowds than do one-day internationals and Twenty20 games. The five-day game has been a victim of the twenty-first-century trend towards instant gratification; the commercial realities of a game that, like all professional sport, depends on television income; and the innocence of those who, because they have not played competitive cricket from their youth, do not appreciate the greater subtleties of the two-innings game.

Too many bland pitches have not helped the cause. I write soon after the 2009 Test series in the Caribbean in which England and the West Indies scored well in excess of 500 runs in four consecutive first innings of the Tests in Antigua and Barbados. The best matches are invariably those played on pitches that allow a balanced contest between batsmen and bowlers. The ideal pitch, indeed, offers some help at different stages of a long match for both fast and spin bowlers. There are commercial reasons for encouraging groundsmen to prepare pitches that last five days, but if that policy produces a dull match it becomes as much a false economy in the long term as preparing bowler-friendly surfaces that create two- or three-day finishes instead.

The ICC, officially the governing body of the world game although in reality a loose confederation of the Test nations, needs firm leadership if a balance is to be restored. The structure of Test cricket needs reorganising. The debilitating struggle between the Indian Premier League and the Indian Cricket League has to be resolved. And, above all, there is an urgent need for the ICC to broker brief windows in a balanced international fixture list for a strictly limited number of domestic Twenty20 leagues.

The overloading of the international programme has been under official discussion for at least ten years. Most of us saw it coming long before that. Given goodwill and decisive leadership, it should not be beyond the powers of administrators to find a better way, based in future, I suggest, on a World Test Championship, played by eight nations over a rolling period of three years.

There would be prize money and sponsorship for each game or series as at present plus an overall bonus, worth more than any other prize in cricket, to go to the nation finishing top on points, and smaller but significant prizes for those finishing second and third, the money to be shared in proportion by cricketers who have played for the top three countries over the three years.

Experiments with floodlit Tests would no doubt have to be sanctioned in some countries where crowds have declined. A strict limit of twelve games or fewer each year for each of the eight nations would have to be imposed, no more than seven of which should be played at home and no more than six between the same nations in any one year. This should not interfere with traditional encounters between, for example, England and Australia or, in times of harmony, India and Pakistan.

The more powerful Test nations should also be able to agree to the demotion of Bangladesh and Zimbabwe from any new World Test Championship, provided that they are given a path back to the top table on merit. Promotion and relegation between various divisions below Test level, along the lines of the hierarchy already well developed by the ICC, would be necessary, offering the hope that one nation might be promoted from one division to the next every three years. Relegation for traditional cricket powers would become an outside possibility too, of course, but it is and always has been a tough game.

Cricket has always been in a state of flux and it will rise above petty trends. It would be the greatest shame, however, if contemporary players who may one day challenge the champions of the past could not be judged for their technique, character, courage and intelligence as well as for the speed of their eyes, feet and hands.

NOTE ON SOURCES

Needless to say to any cricket-lover, *Wisden's Almanacks*, 1863 to 2008, have been the most valuable source of reference for this book. The websites Cricinfo and Cricket Archive have also been very helpful at times. Among general books I had regular recourse to the magisterial *Barclays World of Cricket* (Collins) and my own *World Cricketers* (Oxford University Press). Others that proved very useful included:

Ralph Barker, *Ten Great Bowlers* (Chatto and Windus)
Hilary Beckles, *The Development of West Indies Cricket* (Pluto Press)
Mihir Bose, *A History of Indian Cricket* (Andre Deutsch)
David Frith, *Bodyline Autopsy* (Aurum)
David Frith, *The Fast Men* (Van Nostrand Reinhold)
Steven Lynch, *The Cricinfo Guide to International Cricket 2009* (John Wisden)
Patrick Murphy, *The Centurions* (J.M. Dent and Sons)
R.C. Robertson-Glasgow, *Cricket Prints* (T. Werner Laurie Ltd)
E.W. Swanton, *Cricketers of My Time* (Andre Deutsch)
The Oxford Companion to Australian Cricket (Oxford University Press)
Simon Wilde, *Number One* (Victor Gollancz)

Many of the players I have included have been the subject of biographies. Amongst the more useful were:

John Arlott, *Fred* (Eyre and Spottiswoode)
John Arlott, *Jack Hobbs* (John Murray)
Keith Booth, *George Lohmann* (Sports Books)
Gerald Broadribb, *The Croucher* (Constable)
John Crace, *Wasim and Waqar* (Box Tree)
Gideon Haig, *The Big Ship* (Aurum)
Eric Midwinter, *W.G. Grace* (George Allen and Unwin)
Roland Perry, *Keith Miller* (Aurum)
Irving Rosenwater, *Donald Bradman* (Batsford)
Donald Trelford, *Len Hutton Remembered* (Witherby)
Steve Waugh, *Autobiography* (Michael Joseph)
Simon Wilde, *Ranji* (Kingswood Press)

For obvious reasons I made my list before looking again at John Woodcock's brilliantly succinct little book *100 Greatest Cricketers* (Macmillan), published in 1998, but as time went on I could not resist the occasional peep.